# BELEAGUERED IN PEKING

## THE BOXER'S WAR
## AGAINST THE FOREIGNER

by

### Robert Coltman, Jr., M.D.

Professor of Surgery in Imperial University;
Professor of Anatomy, the Imperial Tung Wen Kuan;
Surgeon, Imperial Maritime Customs;
Surgeon, Imperial Chinese Railways.
Author of "The Chinese, Their Present and Future:
Medical, Political, and Social."

With a New Foreword by Gareth Powell

First published in 1901

Reprinted by
Earnshaw Books
Hong Kong 2008

Beleaguered In Peking

By Robert Coltman, Jr., M.D.

## With a new foreword by Gareth Powell

ISBN-13: 978-988-17326-3-7

*Beleaguered In Peking* was first published in 1901.
This edition with a new foreword is reprinted by
China Economic Review Publishing for Earnshaw Books,
Units C&D, 9/F Neich Tower,
128 Gloucester Road, Wanchai, Hong Kong

This book has been reset in 10pt Book Antigua. Spellings and punctuations are left as in
the original edition.

First printing April 2008
Second printing December 2010

# Contents

# Foreword
## By Gareth Powell

THE Boxer Rebellion in 1899-1900 can be seen as the precursor of modern China. More than any other single event, it initiated the train of circumstances that led to the fall of the Manchu dynasty and created the opportunity for the republican revolution in 1911, succeeded in time by Mao Zedong's communist revolution and from there to China as we know it today.

It was the eruption which finally forced China to come to terms with the existence and technological superiority of the West, and on the positive side, eventually led to a new approach to foreign relations — one not based on an arrogant assumption of superiority for the Middle Kingdom and tributary vassal status for everyone else in the world.

But that is a view that comes with the benefit of a century of hindsight. In terms of the immediate memoir approach, there were several different ways of looking at the upheaval of anti-foreigner feeling that underpinned the Boxer Rebellion, and the author of this first-person memoir of the crisis, Robert Coltman, uses what might be thought of as the Grumpy Old Man approach. In the third sentence of his preface he sets the tone for what is to follow: *I regret that others who had promised me accounts of their work have failed to furnish the promised material.*

But he also nails the true significance of the Boxer Rebellion and the Manchu court's support for it: "The monumental idiocy of the idea that China could successfully defy the whole civilized world was only possible to such brains as those possessed by the densely ignorant Manchus who surrounded the Empress as her cabinet."

First, some information on Coltman. He was an American doctor, born in 1862. He went to China in the mid-1880s, and in 1896 he was appointed professor of anatomy at the Tung Wen College in Beijing (Peking). Two years later, he was appointed professor of surgery at the Imperial University in Beijing, and become the personal physician to the Chinese royal household.

(The accepted spelling of the name of the Chinese capital, then known as Peking, is now Beijing.)

Coltman was also a freelance journalist, writing for the *Chicago Record*. After the Boxer Rebellion had been suppressed, he stayed on in China for another 25 years, becoming an attorney for the Standard Oil Company in the port city of Tianjin (Tientsin) to the south-east of Beijing. He retired in 1925, returned to the United States and died in 1931.

In this book, the second he had written on China, he is virulent in his criticism of the way the Western diplomats in Beijing handled the crisis and absolutely beside himself with rage at Empress Dowager Cixi, the effective ruler of China. But put the grumpiness, which is partly understandable and not at all misplaced, to one side, and the book is revealed as a factual account of one of the most important events in China's history by someone who was there and was a most active participant.

The diary which Coltman, and his young son when he was too busy, kept, is a day by day account of the siege. In places, it is a thriller and you can see why the Rebellion and siege of the legations was made into a successful movie—*55 Days in Peking*.

Towards the end of this book, the author starts listing those people he thought behaved well in the siege. And also those he thought did not. Then he takes an axe to the Empress Dowager Cixi and her reactions to the uprising and finally suggests what he thought must happen in the aftermath (the book was written and published immediately after the Rebellion was suppressed by foreign troops). As it happens, about sixty percent of what he proposed actually came to pass in the decade following.

Robert Coltman spoke Mandarin and this helped him understand what was going on, albeit from a very narrow perspective which, in fairness, he admits to.

In the same way as you would read with some skepticism Princess Der Ling's account of two years in the Forbidden City, in which the author makes the Empress Dowager seem something like a cross between Mary Poppins and Old Mother Riley, so you must read Robert Coltman's account of the siege including the most famous confrontation with the Boxer army, with the thought in mind that this is but one man's view of what happened. Correct in details, but not at all even-handed when dealing with the whole situation.

The Boxer Movement was a rebellion which lasted from November 1899 through to late 1900, although the international agreement wrapping up the incident was not signed until September 7, 1901. Coltman mainly blames the missionaries for making it happen and there is a lot to be said for that view. But it had a wider scope and significance, which was widespread opposition during the final years of the Manchu rule, also known as the Qing Dynasty to all foreign influences.

They were called Boxers because they did exercises not unlike Tai Chi which, they believed, protected them totally from bullets and sword cuts. They were opposed to foreigners as a group but, within that group, they were especially against Christians — Chinese and foreign — and the missionaries who had flooded China.

In June 1900, the Boxers invaded Beijing and generally waged war around the countryside. They killed an unsubstantiated number of non-Chinese — probably over 200 — and tens of thousands of Chinese Christians. The deaths happened mostly in Shandong and Shanxi Provinces as part of the uprising. But there were many in Beijing as well. According to Robert Coltman's figures — and he was in a position to know — there were 49 deaths at the siege itself.

It is a given that it is the victor who gets to write history. In traditional Western histories, the Boxers were condemned as a product of uncivilized, irrational and anti-foreign feelings among the common people. However, in modern Chinese histories, it is not so cut and dried. The Boxers are seen as the catalyst for modern China and could even be praised for being both patriotic and anti-imperialist.

No one argues that when it came to being an army the Boxers were, to put it mildly, farcical. Robert Coltman says that more Boxers died from mis-aimed shots by other Boxers than from anything else.

The Boxer uprising had its origins in Shandong province in 1898, in response to several different events. Three which are often mentioned are the German occupation of the Jiao Zhou region, the British seizing of Weihai city, and the failure of the Imperial court's Self-Strengthening Movement. In fact, the list could be shortened to one—a hatred of Westerners who were plainly trying to take over China for their own purposes.

Possibly the spark was struck in a church in a village in Shandong province where there was a dispute over the property rights of a temple between locals and the Roman Catholic authorities. The Catholics claimed that the temple was originally a church abandoned decades previously and the court ruled in their favor. This caused the villagers, led by the Boxers, to attack the church.

However, Griffith John, who was a long time missionary in China, wrote, after the event, 'It is the height of folly to look at the present movement as anti-missionary. It is anti-missionary as it is anti-everything that is foreign ... The movement is at first and last an anti-foreign movement, and has for its aim the casting out of every foreigner and all his belongings.'

Robert Coltman agrees with this, but still thinks the missionaries have to take a major part of the blame for the eruption.

In January 1900, the Empress Dowager issued edicts in defense of the Boxers. To what extent she did it under pressure from the very conservative officials surrounding her is not clear. What is clear is that this drew heated protests from foreign diplomats.

Meanwhile, the Boxer movement grew in power and in 1900 the Boxers, now joined by elements of the Imperial army, attacked the foreign compounds in the cities of Tianjin and Beijing.

In Beijing, the legations of the United Kingdom, France, Belgium, the Netherlands, the United States, Russia and Japan were all located in the Legation Quarter to the south-east of the Forbidden City. These were linked by the defenders into a fortified compound. The diplomats were still waffling away when the Envoy for the German Empire, Klemens Freiherr von Ketteler, was shot down on June 20 by a Manchu bannerman, marking the start of the siege.

On the one hand, the foreign powers demanded immediate redress. On the other, the Empress Dowager Cixi personally declared war against all Western powers. But, at the time, the power of the court was waning and many regional governors refused to go along. They were supported by a group in Shanghai in resisting the imperial declaration of war.

However, although there was no official declaration of war, this did not end the siege in Beijing which was carried about by the Boxer forces plus a part of the imperial army — the proportions of each are not clear. The fortified legation compound remained under siege from Boxer forces from June 20 to August 14.

This book is about the siege and because it was written as a diary, it has the feeling of absolute authenticity. Reading it, you feel you are at the siege, eating horse-meat and fighting for your life.

The poorly armed and trained Boxer rebels were ultimately unable to break into the legation compound, which was relieved after the famous 55 days by the international army of the Eight-Nation Alliance. The International force reached and occupied Beijing on August 14. After which there was much looting and plunder. German troops in particular were criticized for their enthusiasm in carrying out Kaiser Wilhelm II of Germany's July 27 order: "Make the name German remembered in China for a thousand years so that no Chinaman will ever again dare to even squint at a German."

On September 7, 1901, the Qing court was compelled to sign the "Boxer Protocol", also known as the Peace Agreement between the Eight-Nation Alliance and China. The protocol ordered the execution of ten high-ranking officials linked to the outbreak, and other officials who were found responsible for the slaughter of Westerners in China. China was also fined war reparations of 450,000,000 taels of fine silver.

The imperial government's humiliating failure to defend China against the foreign powers contributed to the growth of nationalist resentment against the "foreigner" Qing dynasty. They were, after all, Manchus.

That wonderfully inspired leader, or raddled evil old harridan, depending on who you believe, Empress Dowager Cixi, had at least some inkling that in order to survive, China had to reform despite her previous views of European encroachment. Soon after the rebellion, the Imperial examination system for government service was eliminated. As a result, the classical system of education was replaced with a Westernized system that led to university degrees. The republican revolution, when it came, was led by a baptized Christian, Sun Yatsen.

This book has been set as the original, warts and all. Only gross spelling and grammatical errors have been corrected. Otherwise this is a facsimile of the original edition.

Gareth Powell, 2008

# Preface

IN the following pages I have endeavored to give an accurate and comprehensive account of the Siege in Peking and of the Boxer movement that led up to it.

Authentic details furnished by representatives of those legations whose work has been specially mentioned have made possible a greater detail in those cases. I regret that others who had promised me accounts of their work have failed to furnish the promised material.

The siege at Pei Tang or North Cathedral, coincident with that of the legations and civilians, is not described for the reason that we were absolutely cut off from them for over sixty days and knew nothing of their movements. Much detail that might be interesting to many I have been obliged to omit, as it would make the book too cumbersome.

I make no claim for the book as a literary effort, the object being to state the facts in the clearest manner possible. The illustrations are from actual photographs, the authenticity of which is absolutely proved, and these carefully studied, add much to the information of the volume.

To my sixteen-year-old son, the youngest soldier to shoulder a rifle during the siege, I am indebted for much of the diary and great help in copying. A considerable portion of the book was written with bullets whistling about us as we sat in the students' library building of the English legation.

There are several men whose work entitles them to decorations from all the countries represented in the siege, and their names will be indelibly written in our memories even if the powers and ministers concerned overlook them. I refer to F.

A. Gamewell, August Chamot, Colonel Shiba, and Herbert G. Squiers.

Robert Coltman, Jr., M.D.
Peking, China, September 10, 1900.

# Chapter I

The author in Chinese dress.

IN the autumn of 1898 in the month of October, very shortly after the famous *coup d'état* of the Empress Dowager of China, an event occurred which may have been the influence that shaped after-events, or it may be that this occurrence was but the premature explosion of a mine being prepared by the Empress and her evil advisers, intended to shake the civilized world at a later date. I refer to the riot at Lukouch'iao, known to the English-speaking world as Marco Polo bridge, from its having been accurately described by that early traveler.

This place had curiously enough been chosen as the northern terminus of the Hangkow-Peking railway, although ten miles west of Peking, and the road consequently is generally known as the Lu Han railway.

The political history of the struggle between the Russian, French and British diplomats in Peking, with reference to obtaining the concession for, and the financing of, this road, is very interesting, and would fill a book of its own; but there is no reason why it should enter into this narrative more than to state that finally the Belgians, acting for Russia and France, obtained the concession to build and finance this greatest trunk line of China.

[1]

To connect this line with the existing Peking-Tientsin railway, a short track was laid from Fengtai, the second station south of Peking, to Lukouch'iao, and a fine iron bridge built over the Hum Ho or Muddy river, a few hundred yards west of the original stone Marco Polo bridge. This short connecting line is but three miles in length, and is the property of the Peking-Tientsin railway.

With this prelude, allow me to proceed with the event with which I was somewhat closely identified, and am able to speak of with knowledge and accuracy.

On October 23 I was called to Fengtai to amputate the leg of a poor coolie, who had been run over by the express train from Tientsin; and after the operation partook of tiffin at the residence of A. G. Cox, resident engineer of the Peking section of the Peking-Tientsin railway. His other guests were Major Radcliffe, of

MARBLE BRIDGE LEADING TO "FORBIDDEN CITY"

A beautiful bridge, which would be a credit to any city. Marco Polo, the great traveler, nearly a thousand years ago described a similar bridge, thus showing how old Chinese civilization is compared with our own.

the Indian army service, on what is known as language-leave in China, and C. W. Campbell, official interpreter of the British legation.

During the meal the newly completed iron bridge was spoken of by Mr. Cox, and we were all invited to accompany him after tiffin on a trolley to inspect the bridge. This I was unable to do, as a professional engagement in Peking in the afternoon at four o'clock prevented.

The next morning I received the following telegram, which should have been delivered the night before; but owing to the closing of the city gates no attempt was made to deliver it:

"Coltman, Peking: — Come to Fengtai at once. Cox and Norregaard both seriously wounded in riot at Lukouch'iao.

"KNOWLES."

I immediately rode in my cart to Machiapu, the Peking terminus of the Peking-Tientsin railway, and wired down to Fengtai for an engine to come and take me down.

In an hour's time I reached Fengtai, and went at once to the residence of Mr. Cox, to find both himself and Captain Norregaard, the resident engineer and builder of the bridge at Lukouch'iao, with bandages about their heads, and a general appearance of having been roughly used. Their story of the riot was told me while I removed the dressings, applied by my assistant, a native medical student of the railway hospital at Fengtai, the day before.

Mr. Cox stated that he and his two guests had gone shortly after tiffin on a trolley to Captain Norregaard's residence, near the bridge, and having added Norregaard to their party, proceeded on foot to the bridge. Near the eastern entrance stood a party of Kansu soldiers, numbering fifty or more, who, upon the approach of the foreigners, saluted them with offensive epithets, in which the well-known "yang kuei tzu" or "foreign devil" was frequently repeated.

Mr. Campbell, who spoke Chinese fluently, remonstrated with the men, and endeavored to have them stand aside and allow the party to cross the bridge; but they obstinately barred the entrance, and warned the foreigners back.

At this juncture a military official of low rank appeared on the track, and Campbell appealed to him to quiet the men, and to allow them to inspect the bridge. This officer replied that the men were not of his company and he had no power over them; but Campbell, knowing well the Chinese nature, at once told him that they should consider him responsible for any trouble, whether he was their particular officer or not.

Upon this the officer ordered the men to open a passage for the foreigners, which they promptly did, and the party of four crossed the bridge. The officer, after they had entered the bridge, left the men and disappeared. They remained a quarter of an hour on the farther side of the bridge and then returned.

As they again neared the eastern side, they saw the same gang of ruffians awaiting them, with stones in their hands, and, upon their arriving within range, were saluted with a volley of stones, many of which took effect. They valiantly charged upon the men, and Cox, being rather severely hit, and spying out the man who had struck him, chased him right into the crowd and knocked him down with a terrific blow. As Cox stands six feet four, and is a remarkably muscular man, this fellow's punishment was severe.

The mob, however, turned upon Cox, who was separated from his companions some thirty odd feet, and, surrounding him, bore him by sheer weight and number to the ground, not, however, before he had placed several of them *hors du combat*.

At this moment Captain Norregaard received a severe stone cut just above his eyes, which severed a small artery and covered his face with blood. Not knowing how dangerously he was wounded, and believing Mr. Cox to be in danger of his life, Norregaard drew his revolver and fired two shots into the mob. The effect was instantaneous. The brutal cowards dropped Cox at once, and ran away like sheep toward their encampment, half a mile distant.

After tying a handkerchief around his head, and assisting Cox to get up, the party hastily ran to the residence of Norregaard and brought Mrs. Norregaard and her eight-year-old son to the trolley, upon which the whole party returned to Fengtai.

Cox then sent a command out by wire for all the engineers working on the Lu Han railway to give up their posts and retire with him to Tientsin to await the settlement of the riot by the Chinese officials, as well as to obtain some guaranty of future good conduct on the part of the government troops, who were yet to arrive from the southwest.

After dressing the wounds of these two gentlemen they took the train for Tientsin, and the writer returned to Peking.

The next day, or two days after the riot, I received a message from Hu Chih-fen, the governor of Peking, requesting me to call upon him at Imbeck's hotel at once. I found the old gentleman with twenty retainers awaiting me. He stated that he had been appointed a special commissioner by the Empress Dowager to proceed to Lukouch'iao and investigate the circumstances connected with the riot two days previously, as well as to inquire minutely into the condition of two wounded soldiers reported by their officers to have been wantonly shot and dangerously hurt by Captain Norregaard. He desired me to accompany him into the camp, and examine the wounds as an expert, so that he could make a proper report to the Empress.

I confess I did not much care to go alone into the camp of the famous Kansu, haters of foreign, but I was under many obligations to Governor Hu, and wanted to oblige him. Besides, there was a spice of adventure about the undertaking that was pleasant to a correspondent. I preferred to go armed, however, as, although knowing a revolver would be of no use in a hostile camp for offensive warfare, yet if Governor Hu remained with me, I reasoned, I could by placing a revolver to his head and holding him hostage prevent any harm to myself—believing as I did that the Empress' special commissioner's person would be sacred in the eyes of her generals. The sequel proved how false this belief was, and that before many hours.

So I requested permission to return home for a moment to obtain a small instrument I might need, as well as to inform my wife of my leaving the city, that she might not be anxious if I did not return until after dark.

Governor Hu replied that I could get whatever instrument I needed at the railway hospital at Fengtai, and that he would send one of his retainers with a message to my wife. I insisted, however, that a return home was imperative, and that I would rejoin him in half an hour. Whereupon he decided to order tiffin in the meantime, and told me to hurry back, take tiffin with him at the hotel, and we would then proceed to Machiapu, where a special train would be waiting for us.

I hastened home, obtained my Smith & Wesson six-shooter, and, after a good tiffin with Governor Hu, rode in a springless cart to Machiapu, entrained, and was speedily at the station at Lukouch'iao.

Upon our alighting from the cars we were met by a sub-official from the camps, and were accompanied by him, and about twenty Kansu soldiers, to the entrance to the railroad bridge, the site of the riot two days before.

Here Hu ordered the bridge watchmen to be brought before him, and he interrogated them as to the occurrences described by Cox and Norregaard. The two watchmen's stories were the exact counterpart of the two foreigners; they agreed in every particular, and placed the whole blame on the Kansu soldiers.

I was surprised at the fearless testimony of these two poor watchmen, one of whom was afterward murdered by the soldiers for testifying against them.

Hu now walked to an inn in the village of Lukou, and told the sub-official to order the general and colonels of all the regiments quartered near-by to appear before him at once, as he would hold an investigation by order of the Empress. He and I drank tea until they arrived.

The first, a General Chang, appeared in about fifteen minutes. We knew some one of importance was coming by the hubbub in the courtyard, the murmur of voices, and the sound of horses' moving feet. Then a soldier appeared in the doorway, and announced:

"General Chang, of the Kansu cavalry, has arrived."

"Ch'ing," replied Hu, and immediately there stood before us as ferocious looking a ruffian as the world could well produce. A tall, weather-beaten man, fifty years of age or more, with rather heavy (for a Chinaman) yet black mustaches, and a more than ordinarily prominent nose; dressed in a dark blue gown, satin high-top boots, official hat with premier button and peacock feather, held at right angles from the rear of his button by an expensive piece of jade. His eyes were deep-set and small, and the whole expression of his face was ferocious and cruel.

He only slightly inclined his head to Hu, took no notice of me, and, ignoring Chinese ceremony, proceeded at once to the highest seat in the little room, and seated himself in the intensely stiff attitude of the god of war one usually sees in a Chinese temple. Hu seemed completely taken aback at this insolence, and allowed the ruffian to remain in the seat of honor throughout the interview.

Before Hu had become acquainted, by his polite questions, with the age, rank, and province of his haughty guest, four other military officers of the rank of colonel and lieutenant-colonel had arrived, namely, Chao, Ma, Wang, and Hung.

Finding their general in the head seat, and noting his imperious bearing, they took their cue from him and maintained throughout the interview the most lofty manner, and treated Hu more like a subordinate than a civil officer of the premier rank and a special high commissioner of Her Majesty the Empress Dowager.

After a few mouthfuls of tea, Hu informed them in most polite and bland terms that as he was Director-General of imperial railways, as well as Governor of the metropolitan prefecture of Shuntienfu, Her August Majesty, the Empress Dowager, etc., etc., etc., had appointed him to visit the general and officers of the Kansu regiments in camp at this place, to inquire into the circumstances of the late riot.

He stated also that he came gladly because he felt that, by careful inquiry into the circumstances, it could doubtless be proved that the soldiers had acted in a rowdy manner without the knowledge and consent of their officers, and that by a well-worded report the latter would escape all blame, and the matter could be settled to the satisfaction of all, especially as no lives had been lost, or imperial property destroyed.

General Chang haughtily replied that it was entirely unnecessary for Hu to come out at all; that Prince Ching had sent a messenger to him in the morning, and the Empress was doubtless aware, through this messenger, of the exact circumstances of the case already, and consequently Hu might as well return and save himself any further trouble.

His impudent manner indicated that, having given his own side of the case to a trusty henchman of Prince Ching's, and obtained that influential prince's partial testimony in his favor, he did not care one way or the other for anything Hu might report later.

But Hu, although very quiet and apparently humble, was firm and determined, and upon the conclusion of Chang's defiant speech, replied:

"It is very well that Her Majesty should have as early a report as possible, and I am glad you have informed her of the events; but as I have been appointed to inquire officially, I should not return without having done my duty, and I hope that none of the officers present will refuse any testimony I require, and compel me to report a lack of respect for Her Majesty's commands."

Chang bit his lips and pulled his mustaches fiercely at this, but said nothing. But Colonel Chao took up the cudgels in a most unexpected manner. Excitedly rising, he commenced a most venomous speech against the introduction of railways into China. He denounced them as the instrumentality of the foreigner to subjugate the country, declaring they had taken away the employment of thousands of carters, boatmen, and wheelbarrow coolies; that they had raised the price of rice and other cereals; that they employed foreigners at high wages, who carried all the money out of the country at the same time that they abused and maltreated the natives under their control, and wound up his rather long discourse by declaring that the abolishing of railways and driving into the sea of every foreigner was the duty of every loyal soldier or subject of the empire.

Hu mildly endeavored to interrupt him several times by telling him that the railways were all Chinese property, and the foreign employees were their Empress' own employees; but Chao drowned Hu's every utterance so that the old man, after several attempts, was, perforce, obliged to keep quiet until the irate colonel had exhausted himself and sat down blowing like a porpoise.

I knew Hu was very unwilling that I should hear all of this speech, which he realized I would perfectly understand, and I felt sure he regretted having brought along a surgeon versed in Chinese.

To me it was a revelation. I had heard that the Mohammedan troops from Kansu, under the famous general Tung Fu Hsiang, were ordered to Peking immediately after the *coup d'état* to support the Empress in her anti-foreign policy. I had heard that they were fanatical, ignorant, and intensely hostile to foreigners. But that they would dare to insult the Empress, in the person of a special commissioner appointed by imperial edict, and reveal the purpose of their general in such open language, and that before a foreigner, I would scarcely have believed short of the testimony of my own ears.

Hu realized that it was useless to attempt to argue with or conciliate these men, and at once set about the object of his visit, as yet unachieved, namely, to find out the condition of the

PAGODA NEAR PEKING

In and around Peking are to be seen many specimens of noble architecture; among which is this beautiful Pagoda, built hundreds of years ago. Such buildings are not erected now, and in some instances they are found standing almost solitary and alone, miles from any great city.

wounded soldiers.

So, upon Colonel Chao's finishing his diatribe, he politely turned to General Chang, without further noticing the enraged colonel, and said:

"I have been told two of your men have been wounded by one of the foreign engineers, and as I have a very skilful surgeon in my employ, who attends to all the people who are injured on the railway, I have brought him along to examine your men, and if you will permit him I am sure he can heal them."

He then introduced me as Man Tai Fu, my Chinese title. They

sullenly acknowledged my presence, for the first time, by a slight nod in my direction, and General Chang asked Hu if he had an interpreter who could converse with me.

"Oh, he doesn't need an interpreter," replied Hu; "he has lived in China fifteen years, has sons and daughters born here, and speaks our language like a native."

Upon this, my nearest neighbor, Lieutenant-Colonel Wang, relaxed a little, and observed that he had never talked with a foreigner, and would be glad to make my acquaintance. I replied that it was a mutual pleasure, and asked his age, province, and personal name, which pleased him greatly.

As it was rapidly growing darker, however, and we had not yet seen the wounded men, Hu cut short our budding conversation by requesting General Chang to show them to me.

He curtly declared, "They are in camp half a mile away, and he can go and see them if he wants to."

"Will you go?" inquired Hu.

"Yes, if you will go with me," I replied, not caring to venture alone into the hostile camp, especially after what I had seen of the temper of their leaders; but I added, "I think it would be much better to have them brought here."

"Yes, yes, that is better," said Hu; but General Chang interrupted him by saying:

"Impossible! they are too ill to be moved, and on this cold day would surely take cold and die."

"Have them well wrapped up and brought quickly," said Hu, without paying attention to the interruption, "for it is getting late, and although I have ordered the city gates not to close until our return to Peking, I am anxious to avoid keeping them open any later than necessary."

General Chang then strode across the room to the door opening into the court, where upwards of three hundred of his men were standing packed like sardines, listening to everything we had been saying, as Chinese custom is, and shouted out: "Bring the two wounded men in here."

Now all of the men had seen Governor Hu snubbed, had heard Colonel Chao revile him and his railroads, and had heard their general say the men would die if brought out in the cold; so, supposing they were to act in a similar way, they, upon receiving this order, held a confab, and a very noisy confab, too, among themselves for a few moments before replying.

As I watched Governor Hu's face grow pale as the commotion increased, I felt that we were in real danger right in the midst of the officers, and that my previous view that I could insure my own safety by threatening Hu's life would avail nothing, as they hated him as much if not more than myself. I could plainly see that I must change my man, and make the general my target if the necessity arose.

Then a voice shouted out from the soldiers almost the exact words of the general.

"They cannot be brought here; the exposure would kill them."

Chang looked at Hu to see what effect this had upon him, but Hu was no coward, and calmly replied: "They must be brought if it kills them; by Her Majesty's commission, I demand it."

The general was bluffing; he sullenly gave in.

"Bring those men at once, dead or alive, you scoundrels," he shouted stentoriously, "and in a hurry, too!"

"Aye, aye," responded a hundred throats, and a number of men left the courtyard at once.

The camp must have been some distance away, for it was over half an hour and nearly candle-lighting time before the two men, each carried on a litter on the shoulders of six men, were brought in.

The first man was covered up in blankets, and pretended to be unconscious; but he proved to have no fever, had a slow pulse, and absolutely no wound but a scratch at the lower end of his right shoulder-blade, which might have been made by a finger-nail, or possibly by a pistol-ball grazing the skin.

The hypocrite Chang bent over me as I was examining, and

asked in a voice of pretended sympathy: "Is he badly hurt? Can he recover? And how long will he be ill?" to which I replied: "Not badly hurt; he will recover; and I will guarantee he is all right day after to-morrow if you will send him at once to my railroad hospital at Fengtai."

I said this, thinking that the British minister in Peking, Sir Claude MacDonald, might be glad to get hold of these men for proper punishment, and that if they were in the hospital at Fengtai they could easily be obtained; otherwise I would have ordered this man to be dismissed at once as shamming.

The second man also pretended to be much worse off than he really was, but he did in fact have a small bullet-wound in his shoulder, from which I extracted with forceps a fragment of blue cotton cloth, and then sent him also to the hospital, predicting his recovery within ten days.

General Chang thanked me for my interest, and promised to reward me for my services when the men recovered; then, nodding coolly to Governor Hu, he and his staff marched out of the inn and left us, and allowed a subordinate to escort us to the special train that brought us down, which was as great a lack of courtesy and positive insult as he could give to the Empress Dowager's high commissioner.

Our return journey was without incident. The city gates were open awaiting us, and were closed immediately upon our entrance. Governor Hu immediately memorialized the throne, stating the result of his inquiries, reported the impudence of Colonel Chao, and made the request that he be turned over to the Board of Punishments for a penalty.

The Empress acknowledged the memorial, and she decided to deprive Colonel Chao of one step in rank, degrading him to a major. This appeared in an edict at once; at the same time she commended Hu for his promptness and general ability.

But, alas for Governor Hu! General Tung Fu Hsiang, the man who was to prove the curse of China, was unacquainted with all these circumstances, and had yet to be heard from. This man had obtained his reputation first as a brigand, and afterward as a leader of Her Majesty's army in putting down a rather formidable rebellion of the Mohammedans in his own province of Kansu. Bold, cruel, and unscrupulous, he had murdered his own provincials, who were but poorly armed and without military discipline, in a most ruthless manner, and had not only suppressed the uprising, but nearly exterminated the rebels.

His fame spread far and wide as a wonderful general, so that when the Empress again assumed power by forcibly seizing the throne from the weak but good-intentioned Kuang Hsu, she decided at once to bring this man Tung and his Kansu ruffians to Peking to assist her in maintaining her authority against all comers. It was en route to Peking that his advance corps, under General Chang, had the trouble at Lukouch'iao.

As soon as Tung Fu Hsiang learned of Colonel Chao's degradation, he was wild with rage, taking the view at once that the insult was not only upon Chao but also upon himself.

Knowing the Empress was in a precarious condition without troops she could depend upon, this courageous adventurer, at his first audience upon his arrival in Peking, promptly told Her Majesty that unless Chao were restored to his rank immediately, and Governor Hu were removed from his offices as Governor of Peking and Director-General of Railways, as well as prevented from taking his seat in the tsung-li-yamen, or foreign office, to which he had just been appointed, he, Tung, would disband his army and return to Kansu at once.

The Empress remonstrated with him in vain, alleging that Hu had only done his duty, and that with his knowledge of foreigners he would be a valuable official in the tsung-li-yamen. But Tung remained obdurate, and the Empress reluctantly yielded and dismissed Hu to private life, where he has ever since remained.

As Governor Hu was alone responsible, by his firm friendship for the English, for obtaining for the Hong Kong and Shanghai banking corporation, an English company, the loan for extending the Peking-Tientsin railway, and had signed the contract which gave the real control of the railway to the English stockholders, his dismissal from office should have been prevented by diplomatic action. As it was, only a mild remonstrance by the diplomatic representative of Great Britain was made, and the tsung-li-yamen passed it, as usual, unheeded. Governor Hu remarked to me a few days after his dismissal, very bitterly, "If I had been the friend to Russia I have been to England I should not now be in disgrace."

He was replaced in the office of Governor of Peking by Ho Yun Nai, and in the office of Director-General of Railways by Hsu Ching Ch'eng, ex-minister to Germany and Russia. The first of these officials was a well-known hater of foreigners, who was suggested by General Tung. The latter was a corrupt opium-eater, already in the pay of Russia, as Chinese president of the Manchurian railway, and was suggested by a high palace eunuch, himself in the pay of Russia.

Tung's influence in Peking now became all-powerful; his soldiers swaggered about the streets in their fancy red and black uniforms, growing daily more menacing to the foreigners they passed, until finally several incipient riots occurred which resulted in one foreigner having several ribs broken and others being assaulted, so that a few of the foreign ministers united and requested that his army corps be removed some distance from the capital. The Empress agreed reluctantly to this, but only sent them a little over a hundred li away.

Tung, early after his arrival, made the acquaintance of Prince Tuan, a stupid, ignorant Manchu, who soon became his complete tool. The question of a successor to the sickly Emperor, Kuang Hsu, had been discussed for several years, as he had as yet no issue, and seemed likely at any time to die childless. The sons of Tuan, of Duke Lan, and of Prince Lien were all considered eligible, and from amongst them must be chosen the future Emperor of China.

Tung saw that Tuan would become his tool much more completely than either of the others, and proposed an alliance between Tuan's son and a daughter of his own, agreeing to support the younger Tuan's candidacy for the throne, with his whole army, if necessary, to accomplish the purpose. Tuan agreed to this, but stated the succession must be made without its being known that he was under obligations to favor Tung's daughter, but that when an apparently open competition for selection of an empress was made, and the various eligible damsels appeared at the court, Tung's daughter should arrive from Kansu in time and be the favored recipient.

On this understanding everything became smooth sailing, and the consummation of their plans, as far as Tuan's interest was concerned, occurred, when in solemn conclave of all the princes of the blood and great ministers of state, on January 24, 1900, Pu Chun, son of Prince Tuan, was solemnly named as successor to the previous emperor, Tung Chih; and poor sickly little Kuang Hsu was succeeded without a successor to himself, but a successor to his uncle being appointed, which, by imperial edict, makes him an interloper.

This was a nice piece of vengeance the Empress Dowager worked out, partly to avenge herself on her nephew for his unsuccessful attempt to shelve her and run his government himself. Tung's intensely anti-foreign sentiments soon made him many friends at court, among the oldest and most conservative Manchus, as well as some of the Chinese. But it was among the former that his influence was greatest.

Many of these men, stupid in the extreme, and too cowardly themselves ever to have originated any of the designs that have since been worked out, joyfully fell in with the plans inspired by his ambition for his own success, but always put forward as for the salvation of his country.

Hsu Ting, Kang Yi, Ch'i Shin, Ch'ung Ch'i, Ch'ung Li, Na T'ung, and Li Ping Heng became his warmest friends and admirers, and formed a cabal which soon controlled the entire administration of government. By Tung's direction all important offices, as they became vacant, or could be readily made so, were to be filled by the Manchu friends of the cabal or, if Chinese, as rarely occurred, then a Chinese who was of their own set and their own creature. This gave them a powerful patronage under their disposal in the lucrative taotaiships and other posts formerly more or less evenly divided between Manchu and Chinese, but now almost entirely limited to Manchus.

Kang Yi was sent on a mission southward through all the provinces to extort money to raise more armies, as well as to feel the pulse of the people in regard to, and encourage them in, their anti-foreign tendencies. Li Ping Heng was sent to examine and report on all the defenses of the Yangtze valley, as well as to denounce any official of progressive tendencies. Yu Hsien was to succeed the latter as Governor of Shantung, and to sow in that province the seeds of disorder and riot that yielded such a bitter crop when they ripened; just as only a poorly-organized, semi-patriotic, but fully looting society could do — an organization that was to be called the I Ho Ch'uan or Boxer organization.

# Chapter II

HSU CHING CHENG
Ex-minister to Germany, member
of Tsung-li-yamen.
Beheaded Aug. 9, for favoring peace.

WITH the appointment of the Manchu Yu Hsien as Governor of Shantung province, to be the successor to the anti-foreign Li Ping Heng, whose removal the Germans had succeeded in effecting, commenced the governmental recognition of the Boxers' society as an agent to expel missionaries, merchants, and diplomats alike. This man, whose hatred of foreigners exceeded that of his predecessor, was no sooner in office than he caused the *literati* all over the province to revive among the masses the "Great Sword" and "Boxer" organizations, which had been a bit shaken by the removal of their encourager, Li Ping Heng.

The foreign residents of Shantung, who had hoped the new government would be an improvement over the old, soon found they were worse off than before. The native Christians were persecuted most bitterly by their heathen neighbors, and their complaints at the yamens treated with disdain.

Yu Hsien did his work thoroughly and rapidly, knowing the foreign power which had compelled the removal of Li Ping Heng would also cause his removal. But as he was only placed in Shantung for the deliberate purpose of making trouble, his removal would mean for him a better post as the reward of his success.

This came when the "Boxers" of Chianfu prefecture attacked and murdered a young missionary of the Church of England named Brookes, who was traveling from Chianfu city to his station of P'ingyin.

The British government demanded his removal from office, and the Chinese government acquiesced; but their treatment of him upon his arrival in Peking alone would have sufficed for an intelligent observer to make clear the policy of the Empress without any other confirmatory evidence, abundance of which, however, was not lacking.

Instead of being reprimanded, we find him granted immediate audience with the Empress, and the next day's Court Gazette informed an astonished world that the Empress had written with her own brush the character "Fu," happiness, and conferred it upon him publicly. Then followed his appointment as Governor of Shansi, a rich mineral province in which the "Peking Syndicate," an Anglo-Italian company promoted by Lord Rothschild, held valuable concessions. In this province, too, were the long-worked missionary establishments of the American Board (Congregationalist) and the China Inland Missions.

The Chinese all understood this as an appreciative approval from the Empress, and so, too, did all the older foreign residents; but the diplomatic corps, beyond a feeble remonstrance from the British and United States ministers, did nothing. So, to-day Yu Hsien is pursuing in Shansi the same policy he did in Shantung, the results of which must turn out similarly.

The Empress appointed as successor to Yu Hsien the man who had turned traitor to the unfortunate young Emperor, Kuang Hsu, Yuan-shih Kai. This man is well known to foreigners. He was formerly Chinese resident at Seoul, and it was largely due to him that the China-Japan war occurred. After the war he was made commanding-general of a force of foreign-drilled troops stationed at Hsiao Chan, south of Tientsin.

Yuan is one of the shrewdest and most unscrupulous men of China, and the Empress, in rewarding him by this appointment for his service to her in making known the Emperor's purpose to send her into captivity, gave power to a man who would desert her, when it suited him, as quickly as he had the weak, but well-meaning, Emperor.

Yuan, upon his arrival in Shantung, found himself in a difficult position. If he encouraged the Boxers he would make enemies of the foreigners. If he was severe with the Boxers he would be removed by the Empress, influenced as she was by General Tung Fu Hsiang and his cabal.

Being a man of great wealth and having a perfect knowledge of the situation, he steered a course that would obviate his striking on either rock. He subscribed to the Boxer organizations where they obeyed him, and punished them where they were refractory, and soon had Shantung, which was in a ferment when he took charge, fairly well in hand.

He gave it to be understood that they would, in time, be able to exterminate foreigners; but they must patiently drill and practice gymnastics until such time as he considered that they had reached perfection, and must not on any account injure a foreigner too early, as it would bring down trouble before the government was prepared to meet it. At the same time he allowed them to pillage and murder the native Christians freely, well knowing this would please the Court, and would not be actively taken up by the foreign powers as an infringement of treaty rights, which it certainly was.

Evidently his idea was, too, that Tung Fu Hsiang's plan to drive out and exterminate all foreigners was an entirely impossible one, and that if he could keep his province from committing any overt act that would lead to a foreign war, for a year's time, the Chihli authorities, all the Manchus, and Tung Fu Hsiang himself would have brought on the war and ruined themselves, while he, Yuan, would then have a chance to cut loose from the conservatives, and come to the front in the new régime, which must come, as a reformer. That he will do this I fearlessly prophesy.

The Boxer organization was not started by Tung Fu Hsiang, but was, by his advice, given imperial sanction and infused with new life and activity. A similar organization, known in olden times in China under the same name, was a volunteer militia for national defense. The recent revival has not only been for defense, but to exterminate the Christian religion and the people who brought it.

That the Chinese people have much to complain of from the aggressive attitude of many native Christians, and particularly the Roman Catholic Christians, no sane man will deny. For years it has been the practice of the priests and of many of the Protestant missionaries to assist their converts in lawsuits against the heathens, and to exert an unjust influence in their behalf. To "get even" with an enemy it is only necessary for a convert to tell his priest or pastor that he has been persecuted in some way for his religious belief, to induce the missionary to take up the cudgel in his defense. I have heard heathen Chinese often assert that these men (converts) appear good enough to their priests, who see very little of their ordinary behavior, but behind the father's back they are overbearing and malicious to all their neighbors, who hate them because they fear them.

After years of residence in China, I have come to the conclusion that it has been a mistake of the Powers to insert in their treaties provisions making the preaching of Christianity a treaty-right, in spite of Chinese objection. Nearly all of the riots in China have come from attempts to force the Chinese officials to stamp deeds conveying property to missionaries for residences or chapels. The animosity incurred in forcing a missionary establishment upon an interior city, town, or village is not obliterated in a lifetime. It may be barely tolerated in time of peace, only to be demolished when the country is disturbed. This applies to the China that has been—barbarian, uncivilized China.

Should the reformers come into power, and religious tolera-
tion be granted as the result of civilization, then there would be
no reason why the missionaries should not work in the more re-
mote parts of the empire; but China, as it has been and is, would
be much more peaceful for all concerned if the proselyting work
was carried on only in the treaty ports. I don't expect any of the
missionary body to agree to this statement, but doubtless many
of their supporters, thinking people, who will take the trouble to
reason it out, will believe it, supported as it is by the testimony
of all the residents of China acquainted with the problem. There
are many reasons for the Chinaman's hatred of the foreigners,
but his religion is the chief one.

In the late riots the railways have been attacked and destroyed, but that came only after a half-year's successful campaign against the converts had led them to want to root out the

INDIVIDUAL EXAMINATION ROOMS FOR CIVIL SERVICE DEGREES
A remarkable feature of Chinese social and political customs is the method of selection for
public office. The candidates for examination are installed in the little rooms or houses shown
in this picture; a supply of water is placed in the large jars at the entrance, and the candidate
is expected, regardless of the pangs of hunger, to remain constantly in this little room until he
shall have passed this examination, which sometimes lass two or three days.

people who brought both the religion and the railways. While I am a Christian myself, and would gladly see China a Christian nation, I cannot help seeing that the policy which has been pursued in forcing Christianity upon the Chinese, in the aggressive manner we have, practically at the point of the sword, has not been a success, and has given to such men as Tung Fu Hsiang a powerful argument with which to persuade his ignorant followers to exterminate alike the foreigner and his converts.

The Boxers are principally of two sorts: the ignorant villager and the city loafer or vagabond. The first easily becomes a fanatical enthusiast; the latter has joined simply to obtain loot. When it became an assured fact that the Empress sanctioned the movement the ranks were rapidly filled, because rewards and preferment were held out as inducements to serve, and the majority of China's population, being poverty-stricken in the extreme, would join any movement that promised an increased income. The Boxer headquarters was the palace of Prince Tuan in Peking. From this place emissaries were sent with instructions, first into Shantung and afterward throughout Chihli, to cooperate with the already-existing secret societies, as well as to organize new companies. Every city, town, and village was visited, the head men consulted, and the young men and boys enrolled.

Their gymnastic exercises, from which they derive their name, were taught them, and they were promised that when they had attained perfection they would be given service under the Empress with good pay and rapid promotion. They were told that if they would go regularly through the ceremonies prescribed every day, in from three to six months they would acquire indomitable courage, and would be invulnerable to bullets and sword-cuts, and that the youngest child would be a match for a grown man of the uninitiated. That thousands believed this nonsense there is no doubt; and thousands of little boys from ten years of age upward eagerly enrolled. The exercise consisted of bowing low to the ground, striking the forehead into the earth three times each toward the east, then south, then throwing themselves upon their backs and lying motionless for several minutes, after which they would throw themselves from side to side a number of times, and, finally rising, go through a number of posturings, as though warding off blows and making passes at an enemy. As a uniform they were given a red turban, a red sash to cross the chest, and red "tae tzio," or wide tape, to tie in the trousers at the ankle.

The time set for their uprising was fixed for the Chinese eighth moon, seventeenth day, being two days after the annual "harvest festival," or pa yueh chieh. The premature explosion of the movement was not anticipated by those who originated it, but it is largely due to its going off at half-cock, so to speak, that enabled the Powers to combat it so readily after they were aware of its existence as a real government agency.

Doubtless the government intended before that time to give arms and ammunition to all grown men; but, in the first place, they were to arm themselves with swords and spears only. They were told, among other things, that at the time of their uprising myriads of regiments of angelic soldiers would descend from the skies to assist them in their righteous war against foreigners.

The Empress herself believed this story as well as the possibility of their being invulnerable to foreign bullets. She is exceedingly superstitious, and in the early part of May consulted the Chinese planchette to read her destiny. Two blind men, holding the instrument under a silk screen, wrote in the prepared sand underneath the following message from the spiritual world:

"Ta Chieh Lin T'ou
Hung Hsieh Hung Liu
Pai Ku Ch'ung Ch'ung
Chin Tsai Chin Ch'in
Tan Kan
T'ieh Ma Tung Hsi Tseu
Shui Shih Shui Fei
Ts'ai pai shiu."

[ 24 ]

The interpretation of this would read in English:

> "The millennium is at hand;
> Blood will flow like a deluge;
> Bleaching bones everywhere
> Will this autumn time be seen.
> Moreover, the iron horse
> Will move from east to west;
> Who's right and who's wrong
> Will then be clearly established."

The millennium is used by the Chinese as a critical period in a cycle of years. The iron horse is supposed to mean war. The Empress understood this to mean that in the war which she intended to commence it would be clearly shown by her success that she was right.

The Boxers, however, completely spoiled all her plans by their eagerness to obtain loot. Being promised the spoil of the foreigners after the contemplated uprising in the eighth moon, they regarded the property of the Christians and their teachers as already mortgaged to them; and, fearful lest the government troops would acquire some of it, they commenced the campaign themselves before the appointed time. How the government at first made feeble efforts to restrain them, and afterward completely gave in and joined with them is now a matter of history.

The monumental idiocy of the idea that China could successfully defy the whole civilized world was only possible to such brains as those possessed by the densely ignorant Manchus who surrounded the Empress as her cabinet. Several of the tsung-li-yamen ministers, like Prince Ch'ing and Liao Shou Heng, weakly tried to reason them out of it, and were promptly given back seats.

Of the others remaining in the tsung-li-yamen after their retirement, none dared say anything against the movement for fear they also would be shelved. But as they were not strong enough to please the Empress in her final dealings with the foreigners, she, a few days before the commencement of the siege, appointed Prince Tuan as head of the yamen, in place of Prince Ch'ing, and at the same time appointed two fire-eating foreign-haters, Chi Shui and Na T'ung, to seats in that obstructive body. These men, with Tung Fu Hsiang and the cabinet, must be held responsible for the murders of Baron von Ketteler, F. Huberty James, David Oliphant, H. Warren, Ed Wagner, and the other civilians and guards killed during the siege, as well as for many missionaries in the province that have doubtless perished, but of whose fate we, being besieged, had no certain knowledge.

That the Powers, in the settlement of their crimes, will treat them as murderers, as they are, we can scarcely doubt, and we hope none of them in any way implicated will be allowed to escape capital punishment.

# Chapter III

CHUNG LI
Manchu Boxer Chief

THE murder of the Church of England missionary, Brookes, in Chinanfu prefecture, Shantung province, by the Boxers, was the beginning of the explosion. On January 4, 1900, I cabled home the occurrence of the murder. On January 5 I cabled that the Americans in Taianfu, two days' journey by cart south of the scene of the murder, were in danger, and that the United States minister had requested that they be protected; also that the Empress Dowager had expressed to Sir Claude MacDonald, through the tsung-li-yamen, her horror at the deed, and from thenceforth, under the respective dates given below, I sent cables recording the Boxer progress.

January 13. Christians in Shantung are being constantly pillaged by marauding parties of Boxers. The Taianfu district is especially dangerous, as the prefect will not allow them to be interfered with. Dr. Smith, of Pang Chuang, in northern Shantung, has also written and telegraphed the United States legation that matters in his district are in the same condition. Christians murdered, chapels burned and looted, and no redress obtainable from the officials.

January 15. An imperial edict was issued yesterday which really commends the Boxers, and is sure to cause trouble. Upon Baron von Ketteler representing this to the tsung-li-yamen he was given no satisfactory answer to account for it.

January 24. Boxer movement is rapidly spreading, and the situation fills many with alarm. Prince Tuan's son has been chosen as the successor to the Emperor, which is an unfavorable omen.

January 25. An edict has been promulgated apparently from the Emperor, but really from the Empress Dowager, stating that, because of his childless condition and infirm health, he has decided for the good of the state to appoint Pu Chun, son of Prince Tuan, as his successor.

February 5. Although the Boxer movement continues to increase in the northern provinces, Peking remains quiet.

February 10. The anti-foreign crusade is proceeding apace. Jung Lu, Hsu Tung and Kang Yi have assumed great power, and are constantly with the Empress. The Boer successes in the Transvaal are being used to show the masses that a very little country can defy a big government if only the hearts of the people are in the struggle. British prestige here declining rapidly as a consequence. A Boxer mob has attacked the Germans building the railway in Shantung, and driven the foreigners away from their work. As Baron von Ketteler insists upon their going on with the work, the tsung-li-yamen finds it difficult to please both the throne and the foreigners.

February 12. A letter received from a Presbyterian missionary in Chinanfu states that over seventy families of Christians have been mobbed and looted in his district, and that they can obtain no redress from the local officials, and that the Boxers, knowing this, are rapidly increasing and growing bolder.

February 15. Imperial edict orders the suspension of any native papers showing reform tendency, and the editors to be imprisoned.

February 19. The annual audience with the foreign ministers took place with most scant ceremony and in a shabby apartment.

ANCIENT ASTRONOMICAL INSTRUMENTS

These peculiar instruments, which are of great astronomical merit, were made during the reign of Kublai Khan, A. D. 1264. An especial interest attaches to this illustration, on account of the attempt of the Germans to remove these instruments to Berlin, and the protest made against it by General Chaffee, of the U.S. Army. The engraving shows the instruments just as they were used for hundreds of years, before they were taken apart for removal to Europe.

This was done with the direct purpose of insulting them, but none remonstrated.

February 23. A French priest from Tientsin informs me that all that district is pervaded by the Boxers, who openly avow they are drilling to come to Peking and drive out and exterminate all foreigners.

February 25. Several thousand armed Boxers have possession of the German railway building at Kaomi in Shantung, and state their purpose is to drive out the foreigner.

February 28. Yuan Shih Kai, Governor of Shantung, has sent a private messenger, an ex-drillmaster in his army corps, to Baron von Ketteler, the German minister, to say he will disperse the Boxers at Kaomi and restore quiet.

March 14. The man who obtained for the British syndicate the concession known as the Peking syndicate's Shansi concessions to mine and build railways, was arrested for assisting foreigners to obtain concessions in China. Upon Sir Claude MacDonald's demanding his release, the Empress promptly sentenced him to imprisonment for life. This will deter others from helping foreigners in any capacity.

March 15. United States Minister Conger, having protested against the Empress using Yu Hsien, ex-governor of Shantung, in any province where American interests are great, is greatly displeased to learn to-day that, so far from heeding, the Empress has actually appointed him Governor of Shansi, in which are not only a number of American missionary stations, but the interests of the Peking syndicate.

April 24. Boxers aggregating nearly 10,000 have collected in one place near Paotingfu, and are very disorderly. The outlook is very threatening, not only there but at Tungchow, thirteen miles south of Peking, and at Tsunhua, to the east of Peking. At all these places there are large American missionary stations.

May 17. Boxer movement has now assumed definite shape and alarming proportions. They have destroyed several Catholic villages east of Paotingfu, and are moving on the property of the American Board's mission at Choochow at Kung Tsun. They have also looted the London mission's premises, and killed several Christians. Boxers are now daily to be seen practicing in Peking and the suburbs. Situation is growing serious here.

May 18. I have been warned by one of the princes that I should take my family from Peking, as he states his own elder brother is a Boxer, and that foreigners are no longer safe in Peking. Have fully informed the United States minister of the situation, but he believes the official promises that all is well.

May 21. Foreign ministers have held a meeting and discussed question of bringing legation guards to Peking. The French minister favored this, but Conger opposed, stating he believed the government resolutely means to suppress the Boxers. No action was taken, it being decided to await further developments.

May 24. The tsung-li-yamen has not yet replied to the joint note sent them by the foreign ministers four days ago, requesting that the Boxers be dealt with summarily. Unless an immediate and vigorous foreign pressure is applied, a general uprising is sure.

May 25. General Yang was killed at Tinghsing, Hsien, near Paotingfu, either by his own soldiers or the Boxers. The soldiers then joined the Boxers.

May 26. The tsung-li-yamen has sent a vague and temporizing reply to the foreign ministers' demand requiring the suppression of the Boxers. They are now regularly enrolled at the residences of several of the princes in this city.

May 28, A.M. The foreign ministers held another meeting today, but still deferred any action looking toward defense, as the tsung-li-yamen promises that it will shortly issue a strong edict that will suppress the Boxers. Pichon distrusts the Chinese promises and again advocates strong legation guards.

FAMOUS ARCH OF THE MING TOMBS

A celebrated traveler has said that it was worth encircling the earth to see this beautiful piece of architecture. Were it in the middle of Paris or New York, it would arouse great admiration and wonder; but, situated as it is in the midst of a wild and barren landscape, with huge mountains for a background, and representing as it does, the burial place of a mighty dynasty that for ages ruled a stupendous nation, it fills the beholder not only with wonder and admiration, but with awe.

May 28, 4.10 P.M. Boxers have burned the bridge and destroyed the track at Liuliho, forty five miles west of Peking, on the Lu Han railway, and are advancing toward Marco Polo bridge, twelve miles from here. The foreigners employed on the railway have all fled. The Tientsin train is overdue, and our communication with the coast threatened. The legations are just beginning to wake up to the fact that the Boxer movement is a perilous one.

May 29. At last it has come to our very door. Not only Liuliho and Changhsintien, on the Lu Han railroad, have been destroyed, but the junction at Fengtai, only six miles from here, has been attacked, looted, and burned, and all the foreign employees have fled to Tientsin. The foreign ministers now want guards badly, but, as it is not yet known whether the railroad is torn up at Fengtai, there is no certainty of getting them quickly. The fate of a large party of French and Belgian women and children, known to reside at Changhsintien, is not known. Legation street is crowded with villainous-looking ruffians congregating to loot if opportunity offers. Until troops arrive the situation is precarious.

May 30. The tsung-li-yamen has requested the foreign ministers not to bring troops, assuring them they are not necessary; but the situation here has at last impressed them, and they have disregarded the yamen and ordered up guards at once. The populace are quite excited, and only need a slight cause to break out.

May 30, P.M. Viceroy of Chihli has forbidden guards taking train at Tientsin. Fifteen warships are reported at Taku.

May 31. Viceroy of Chihli has been ordered by the yamen to allow guards to take train for Peking, but requested ministers to bring only small guards, as last year. Troops have arrived.

June 1. Populace seems cowed and sullen. Riots in the city may now be prevented, but the problem of dealing with the movement is one requiring active diplomatic effort.

June 2. Station buildings south of Paotingfu on the Lu Han

railway have been burned, and railroad destroyed. Party of thirty Belgians, including women and children, attempted to escape to Tientsin, and were attacked by Boxers. Several known to be killed; fate of remainder unknown. Said to be surrounded when their native interpreter left to obtain help. Native Christians of the American Board's mission at Choochow, and the American Presbyterian mission at Kuanhsien, are pouring steadily into Peking, to escape murder at the hands of the Boxers. All their houses have been looted and burned.

June 2, 8 P.M. Serious dissension among Chinese ministers, Prince Ching favoring moderation and suppression of the Boxers. He is said to be secretly supported in this by Jung Lu and the tsung-li-yamen. Prince Tuan, supported by Hsu Tung, Kang Yi, and other intensely anti-foreign ministers, is favoring the Boxer movement. A crisis is imminent.

June 3. Church of England missionaries Robinson and Norman killed at Yungching by Boxers, and their chapels looted and burned. Boxers now have entire control of country from Tientsin to Paotingfu, and thence northeastward to Peking; native troops make no effort to suppress them. All religious and missionary work in North China is ended unless treaty powers compel observance of treaty provisions, and demand indemnities for each and every infringement.

June 4. Native converts from the west of Peking report that many thousand Boxers are assembling at Choochow preparing to attack the foreigners and converts in Peking. The missionaries are convinced of the truth of this, and have informed their legations, who will not believe it. Dr. Taylor, of the American Presbyterian mission at Paotingfu, telegraphed to the American minister: "We are safe at present, but prospects threatening."

June 4 (afternoon). Morning train arrived from Tientsin four hours late, owing to burning of bridge and destruction of station building at Huangtsun by Boxers. Noon train now overdue, and, as the telegraph wires have been cut, is unheard from. Unless foreign troops are immediately placed to guard the railway we shall be cut off from help by way of the sea.

June 5. The American missionaries in Paotingfu have been attacked, and have wired for help. The tsung-li-yamen, when appealed to by United States minister, said it would telegraph the local officials to do so. But unless a relief party rescues them speedily their fate is certain death.

June 5, P.M. American Methodist mission at Tsunhua, with twelve children and four women, are beset and have wired for help. Trains from Tientsin have ceased to arrive; we are sending a courier overland with mails.

June 6. United States consul at Tientsin has wired the minister here that the Tientsin native city is in great excitement, and the situation is very serious; he advised that no women or children attempt to enter Tientsin from Peking, as they could not get through. Fate of Paotingfu missionaries unknown, as we can get no telegrams through.

June 6, P.M. United States consul wires from Tientsin that the situation there is growing steadily worse; an attack is imminent. Here in Peking we are all collecting in the legations, but have insufficient arms and ammunition. Nevertheless we will make a determined stand.

June 7. I have overwhelming evidence that government officials are the real causes of the Boxer movement, acting under the direction of the Empress. Therefore the tsung-li-yamen and cabinet are supporting this movement, which is intended to exterminate all foreigners and Christian converts. The senile cabinet has persuaded the Empress this is possible, and they are quite willing to face the inevitable foreign war that their policy entails. The imbecility of this idea does not in any way interfere with the facts. The foreign powers should all prepare for war at once, or entrust the work to those powers nearest and best fitted to successfully undertake it. The sooner this is done the less will be the loss of life and property. The tsung-li-yamen yesterday promised Sir Claude MacDonald, through the secretary of Prince Ching, that if the foreign ministers would not press for a personal audience with the Empress, as they intended doing, Prince Ching would guarantee the restoration of the interrupted railway in two days, and a general amelioration of the condition of affairs. Another useless edict was put out to-day mildly enjoining officials to distinguish between good and bad Boxers, and punish only the bad.

June 7, P.M. Twenty converts have been murdered at Huang-tsun, thirteen miles south. Missionaries at Tungchow have decided to abandon their valuable compound, and have telegraphed the United States minister to send them a guard of marines to escort the women and children to Peking. This compound contains a valuable college, and will inevitably be burned.

June 8. Tungchow missionaries have arrived safely in Peking. Two other stations on the Tientsin railway, Lofa and Langfang, have been burned, as well as the college compound at Tungchow. Tsung-li-yamen has refused to allow a reinforcement of the legation guards now in Peking. Although thirty warships of all nationalities are at Taku, Peking is completely isolated. Why America, after Secretary Hay's much vaunted open-door policy, should allow her representative to be denied sufficient guard for the safety of himself and his countrymen is something one cannot comprehend, unless the representative has not kept his government well informed.

June 8, P.M. Most alarming situation. Missionaries from all compounds in this city compelled to abandon their homes and seek refuge in the Methodist mission, which is nearer the legations, being a half mile east of the United States legation. They have a few shotguns and very little ammunition, and are surrounded by their terrified converts, who have fled with them. Prince Ching's promise of restored railway has proved false. The foreign ministers now realize they have been fooled again, and have lost two days' valuable time. We call upon our government to make haste and rescue our wives and families quickly or it will be too late.

June 9. Emperor and Empress return to-day to the city from

the summer palace. Another futile edict has been put out to further delude the foreign ministers. It is known that Prince Ching has expostulated with the cabinet, but to no purpose.

June 9, P.M. United States Minister Conger has sent in all twenty marines to assist the Methodist mission compound in their defense. Still no word from Paotingfu missionaries.

June 10. Five hundred marines and sailors left Tientsin to relieve us. They can get as far as Anting, twenty miles south of here, by train, and will then have to march the remainder of the distance. If prompt they should arrive tomorrow. Methodist mission is fortifying the place with strong brick walls and barbed wire.

After this telegram I was notified that the wires south were cut, and sent only one message more, on July 12, by way of Kiachta, relating the murder of the Japanese secretary and urging prompt government action looking to our rescue.

The history of the growth of the Boxer movement seems to me to have been clearly shown by these telegrams, so that any one of ordinary understanding could have been, by June 1, if in possession of this series of dispatches, fully acquainted with the situation.

The United States minister, the British minister, and the French minister were each acquainted with all the above major facts and much more minor detail.

# Chapter IV

*Diary of the author from June 1 to June 20*

CHAO SHU CHIAO
Boxer Member of Cabinet

THE following transcription of my diary gives the principal events in the situation up to the date of the close siege, going back a little in point of time from the last chapter.

June 1. After three days of exciting mental strain, we can at last breathe easier. Rumors continue to fill the air of plots within the palace, riots against the Catholic cathedral, railway being torn up between here and Tientsin, etc. But the solid fact remains that a few foreign guards have arrived at six legations, and a machine gun will now have something to say in one's behalf if the excited populace's thirst for foreign blood becomes too pressing.

With the exception of M. Pichon, the French minister, all the other ministers are greatly to blame for their tardy recognition of the impending trouble, and they have very nearly had the odium of a preventible foreign massacre to answer for.

Sir Claude MacDonald, for whom the entire English community outside his legation feel, and have openly expressed, the greatest contempt, would not believe that there was any danger coming, and vigorously opposed Pichon's advice that the troops be sent for ten days ago.

Mr. Conger seconded Sir Claude, partly because the United

States legation quarters are so limited that the second secretary and his wife are obliged to live in two rooms over the main office building, and partly because he believed the government willing and capable of putting down the disorder. Both were suddenly converted when Fengtai, only six miles away, was burned, and the Boxers were reported marching unopposed upon Peking. Then the most exciting telegraphing for warships to come to Taku, and guards and machine guns to come to Peking, became the order of the day.

Had the Boxers been at all organized they could have torn up the track for a mile or two at Fengtai, and effectually cut off the troops from arriving in time to prevent any city riots. Fortunately, they seem to have been carried away by the desire to loot, and after they had carried off all the furniture and belongings of the eight foreign residences at Fengtai, and robbed the Empress' private car of all movable property, they were content to set fire to the stations and machine shops, and then clear out home to the adjoining villages.

June 4. None of the Boxers have been punished, and they have grown bolder, burning the next station below Fengtai, known as Huangtsun, thirteen miles from Peking, killing two Church of England missionaries named Robinson and Norman at Yungching, and defeating a force of Cossacks sent out from Tientsin to search for the surviving Belgians escaping from the Lu Han railway. In spite of this, and with seventeen men-of-war at Tangku, the foreign ministers, besides bringing up each a guard of fifty or seventy-five men to protect his own legation, are doing nothing—that we can see at any rate—to pacify the country. Why they don't land a large force, come to Peking, and seize the old reprobates that they all know are the real bosses of the Boxer movement in Peking, and hold them responsible for any further movement, nobody knows.

Every minister can tell you that Hsu Tung, Kang Yi, Chung Li, Chung Chi, and Chao Shu Chiao, with Prince Tuan, are the real causes of all the present disorder. Although they all know this, they still pretend to believe the assurances of the government to the contrary. . . .

June 13. Events have been too exciting to allow of one sitting down quietly to write. The missionaries from Tungchow, thirteen miles south of Peking, have fled into this city, and all their college plant, private residences, and property have been destroyed by soldiers sent from the taotai's yamen to protect them. All the Peking missionaries have gathered together in the Methodist mission compound, where, with such arms as they could collect — a few shotguns, rifles, and revolvers — and with a guard of twenty marines, sent by Mr. Conger, United States minister, they have fortified themselves with barbed wire and brick fences, and are "holding the fort."

For days we have heard no word from our Presbyterian missionaries at Paotingfu. The last word, now some days since, which came through the tsung-li-yamen and is therefore untrustworthy, was that they were safe at present. Wires south have been cut since the burning of the college buildings at Tungchow, and I have been unable to write home the developments daily occurring.

On the 10th of June, just before the wires were cut, we had a message from United States Consul Ragsdale, saying eight hundred odd troops were coming to our assistance, but to-day is the fourth day since its receipt, and we only know of their reaching Lofa, a burned station on the railway to Tientsin, on Monday night. We have been expecting them every hour since, but no definite word of their arrival at any other place has reached us. Why they don't send natives in advance we can't imagine.

June 18. Eleven days we have been besieged in Legation street. Our little guard of four hundred and fifty marines and sailors of all nationalities have kept unceasing watch night and day, and are nearly exhausted. Eleven days ago we were told that an army was marching to our relief, and although they had only eight miles to come we have not yet seen them, nor do we know their whereabouts.

We have nightly repelled attacks of Boxers and soldiers of the government, and have killed in sorties over two hundred of them; but we have millions about us, and unless relieved must soon succumb. Our messengers to the outside world have been captured and killed, and our desperate situation, while it may be guessed, cannot be truly known.

With fifty men-of-war now at Taku we have to remain within our barricaded streets and witness the destruction of all the mission premises and private foreign residences on the outside.

The American Board mission's large property, the two large Catholic cathedrals known as the South cathedral and the East cathedral, the two compounds of the American Presbyterian mission, the Society for Propagation of the Gospel mission, the International Institute, and the London mission have all furnished magnificent conflagrations, which we have beheld without being able in any way to prevent.

At each place the furious Boxers, aided by their soldier sympathizers, have murdered, with shocking mutilation, all the gatekeepers as well as any women and children in the neighborhood suspected of being Christians or foreign sympathizers.

At the South cathedral the massacre was shocking; so much so that when some of the poor mutilated children came fleeing across the city, bringing the news of what was going on, a relief party was organized from our little force, consisting of twelve Russians, twelve American marines, and two civilians, W. N. Pethick and M. Duysberg, armed with shotguns, who, risking conflict with the Manchu troops, marched two miles from our barricades and, coming on the Boxers suddenly in the midst of the ruins, fired a number of volleys into them, killing over sixty, upon which the rest fled. They then collected the women and children hidden in the surrounding alleys, and marched them back to us, where they are for the present safe.

I have just finished dressing the wounded head of a little girl ten years of age, who, in spite of a sword cut four inches long in the back of her head and two fractures of the outer table of the skull, walked all the way back here, leading a little sister of eight and a brother of four. As she patiently endured the stitching of the wound, she described to me the murder of her father and mother and the looting of her home. One old man of sixty carried his mother of eighty upon his back and brought her into temporary safety; but how long before we are all murdered we cannot say.

Our anxiety has been something frightful, and at this moment, many days since we were told that troops were coming to our relief, we are apparently no nearer rescue than at first. We can't comprehend it. Night before last, after being driven away by our hot rifle fire, the Boxers turned on the defenseless shopkeepers in the southern city, and burned many acres of the best business places and native banks.

They also burned the great city gate, known as the Chien Men, an imposing structure of many stories high, which must have il-

MAIN GATE TO PEKING, DESTROYED BY BOXERS SEPT. 16, 1900

This is one of Peking's main and most imposing gates. Notice the massive building above the wall; note the solidity of the wall itself; an idea of its great height can be formed by noticing how small a proportion is occupied by the arch and yet how small a proportion of the arch is actually required for the passing vehicles.

luminated the surrounding country for miles. Surely our troops must have seen the glare, if they were within forty miles of us. We begin to fear they have met with an overwhelming force of Chinese soldiers, and have been driven back to Tientsin.

The tsung-li-yamen, or foreign office, is utterly powerless, and yet it continues to send us messages stating it is going to protect us, and it has the Empress issue daily edicts, which, while apparently condemning the Boxers, really encourage them.

The Manchu soldiers have stood idly by in thousands, and have seen the frightful butcheries of converts and suspected converts, without raising a finger to interfere. When questioned why they did not obey the edicts authorizing them to repress arson and looting they have replied, "We have other instructions."

Mauser bullets are nightly fired at our sentries, and every night we have to turn out a number of times to repel the cowardly natives, whom we find sneaking down upon us, and who dare attack only under cover of darkness.

The behavior of our women and children under these circumstances has been remarkable, and their courage and bravery above all praise.

Should these lines ever be published I wish to make known to the world the great courage, devotion, and constant watchfulness of Captain John T. Myers, of the Marine Corps. We will owe to him our lives and the lives of our loved ones if we are ever rescued. His bravery and endurance will, if he survives, mark him for high command some day. While all the officers here have acted well, yet he is head and shoulders above them in coolness and decision, and all the other nationalities come to him for advice and counsel.

He is well seconded here by ex-Lieutenant Herbert G. Squiers, Seventh United States Cavalry, who is first secretary of legation. Had Mr. Squiers been minister, we would never have been in our present terrible situation, for he realized the appalling nature of the threatened outbreak while the ministers pooh-poohed it. As he could not of his own initiative order up troops in time, he laid in abundant stores of rice and other eatables, and bought up all the wagons and ammunition purchasable.

The blind trust the ministers (with the exception perhaps of M. Pichon) placed in the promises of the tsung-li-yamen, in the face of the daily increasing riots and murder, is an instance of childlike simplicity which I trust they may never have an opportunity to repeat elsewhere. The entire community here, of civilians and military alike, condemn them as a set of incompetents.

They now, of course, all see their mistake in being fooled by the tsung-li-yamen, and prevented from bringing a sufficient force here until the railroad was destroyed and hordes of fierce Kansu ruffians placed in the way of advancing relief.

The marines of the Newark and Oregon, of which we have fifty, that compose the entire American force, are a sturdy lot of courageous, devoted men. Sober, intelligent, cheerful, enduring, all of them are as brave as lions. Sergeant Walker alone, at the South cathedral, killed seven of the Boxers.

The district held by us is about a half-mile east and west on Legation street, and is guarded by blocking the streets at the Italian legation on the east and the Russian legation on the west. At each barricade there is placed a machine gun. A diagram of the ground held will be found on another page. June 19, yesterday, the tsung-li-yamen ministers (four of them) visited the English, Russian, and American legations, and begged the foreign ministers to persuade the relief guards that we hope are coming to our aid, to return, assuring them that from this time on the Chinese would prevent any further Boxer outrages on foreigners, and that legation premises should be safe. They also said the Empress was now sure that the Boxer movement was a menace to the government as well as the foreigners, and that the imperial troops would be ordered to shoot every Boxer on sight. As all the afternoon our sentinels on the city wall saw Boxers in full regalia going at pleasure among the native troops stationed about the ruined Chien Men, we know that the tsung-li-yamen's words were, as usual, a pack of lies.

A messenger arrived yesterday from Tientsin from Mr. E. B. Drew, commissioner of customs, to Dr. Morrison, of the London *Times*, stating that the railroad had been destroyed in the rear of the relief column, and they were being driven back on Tientsin and away from us.

Surely our condition is desperate. Food is getting scarce. Boxers are mixing openly with the Chinese soldiers, our own soldier boys are getting worn out by constant watching, and no help is nigh.

July 18. On June 19, nearly a month ago to-day, the tsungli-yamen sent the foreign ministers word that, as the admirals at Taku had notified the viceroy of Chihli through the French consul if he opposed troops landing in any required numbers they would take the Taku forts, and as this was really a declaration of war, the foreign ministers were hereby requested to leave Peking, one and all, within twenty-four hours, and proceed to Tientsin en route to their respective countries, a Chinese escort for which was to be provided by the Chinese government.

As the railroad had already been destroyed all the way to Tientsin, and the intended relief corps under Admiral Seymour and Captain McCalla had been driven back without being able to reach us, and as we knew the country between Peking and Tientsin was filled with thousands of Boxers and hostile soldiers, it seemed patent to the most simple intellect that to leave the protection of our legation walls was to invite massacre.

But the intensely dense ministers, Sir Claude MacDonald, E. H. Conger, M. de Giers, M. Pichon, and others, all excepting Baron von Ketteler, the German minister, actually agreed to proceed to Tientsin on the morrow with all their nationals, providing only that the Chinese government would furnish transportation. The military officers all declared this would mean the massacre of the entire community.

The ministers, however, would certainly have had us all thus massacred had not the unfortunate Baron von Ketteler been murdered the next morning by the Chinese troops while proceeding to the tsung-li-yamen to consult about details. He rode, as is customary, to the tsung-li-yamen from his legation in a sedan chair. When passing the entrance of Tsung Pu street, just below the yamen, he was fired upon by a troop of Manchu troops of Yung Lu upon the command of a lieutenant with a white button, and was mortally wounded. His secretary interpreter, Mr. Corder, who accompanied him, was also badly wounded by the volley, but, aided by some friendly natives, managed to escape to the Methodist mission near Legation street, where, after having his wounds dressed, he was sent on to his legation. The horse coolie had already quickly galloped back to the legation and given the alarm.

The folly of trusting our lives to the Chinese escort was thus made clear, and the foreign ministers, dense as they were, could not but realize that to trust themselves and their families to the tender mercies of the ruffians who would be appointed to escort

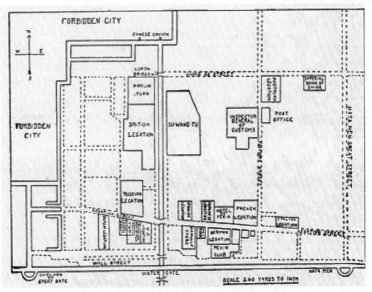

GROUND-PLAN OF THE FOREIGN LEGATIONS IN PEKING
This will serve to locate the various buildings pictured elsewhere.

and murder them and us, would be lunacy to a degree at which even they were not yet arrived.

I had, in company with the correspondent of the London *Times*, early in the morning of the 20th of June, in the most emphatic language, represented the true state of the case to Minister Conger, only to be met with the cold reply, as he turned away after listening to us, "I don't agree with you."

But on receipt of the news of Ketteler's death, a few moments later, the United States minister "changed his mind," and reluctantly admitted it would be impossible to go to Tientsin, and that we must try and defend ourselves in Peking until a large relief force could arrive to rescue us.

Hasty preparations were then made to send all the women and children into the English legation, which was the largest of all the legations, as well as the strongest, from which to make a final stand.

In a few hours after the news of Von Ketteler's murder a steady stream of men, women, and children, carrying bundles, buckets, and trunks, could have been seen pouring into the main gate of the British legation, all with anxious faces. Carts, too, loaded with provisions from the three foreign stores, were making the best use of the time in transferring all the available eatables and drinkables within the protection of the legation walls.

As the twenty-four hours granted us in which to hasten from the city expired at 4 P.M., all used their entire energy as well as that of the coolies and servants at their disposal, so that at the time specified, when the Chinese opened a terrifying fire upon us from all sides, provisions enough to last us several months were safely under shelter.

# Chapter V

HSII YUNG I
Beheaded for favoring moderation.
Member of Tsung-li-yamen.

AT four o'clock on the afternoon of June 20, 1900, all the foreign women and children, and nearly all of the civilians of Peking and vicinity, including the customs staff and the missionary body, had taken refuge in the British legation. It was surprising to every one to find that, in the time that had elapsed since the arrival of the British marines, May 31, no barricades had been erected, no trenches dug, nor any attention paid whatever to rendering the place better able to stand a siege.

In talking with one of the British sergeants, and commenting upon this utter neglect, he informed me that Captain Halliday had, a few days before, attempted to improvise some barriers by means of dry-goods boxes filled with earth, but had been so laughed at and snubbed by Captains Strouts and Wray, British officers, that he had given up the attempt.

Sir Claude MacDonald, the British minister, who is an ex-major in the army, and should have instructed in this very important duty, was, equally with marine officers, culpably silent.

The American missionaries, however, no sooner arrived than they formed committees on fortification, sanitation, food, etc., and set actively to work; and to them belongs, as every one agrees, the credit of placing the legation in a defensible condition.

To Mr. F. D. Gamewell, of the American Methodist mission, more than to any other one man, is due the success which has attended our defense. His energy was simply extraordinary. From morning until night he was to be seen superintending the filling of sand-bags, the tearing down of houses adjoining our walls that might serve as cover to the enemy, the building of barricades and strengthening of walls from the timbers and brick so obtained, making loopholes at the proper places for firing through and doing, in fact, everything that could have been done by an army engineer of experience; all the time, too, under a galling rifle fire from the outside Chinese army, under the command of the Kansu ruffian, General Tung Fu Hsiang.

All the Chinese coolies, servants, cooks, and retainers of the foreigners, to the number of over 1,000, were enrolled, given a badge sewed to their sleeves, declaring their identity, and hours fixed for their employment on public works for general defense.

Latrines and garbage tanks were arranged, and the place put under proper sanitary regulation, supervised by Drs. Coltman, Lowry, and Inglis.

A hospital was equipped under Doctors Velde and Poole, and a trained nurse corps installed, consisting of several lady physicians and three trained nurses.

The Holland and Belgian legations, being outside of the line of defense adopted by consultation of the military captains, were abandoned, but it was decided by the military to hold the French, German, American, Italian, and Russian legations, until absolutely untenable.

With the exception of the Italian legation, these premises are still in our possession, although the French and German legations are but shattered wrecks, every building being full of holes from shells and round-shot of the Chinese cannon, often fired at only two hundred yards' distance.

On the afternoon of that first day of the siege, F. Huberty

James, professor of English in the Imperial University, noticed several Chinese soldiers upon the bridge, a few hundred yards north of the legation gate. Without stating his motive to any one, although it is supposed he intended to converse with them, and, if possible, find out their orders in regard to us, he walked from the gate up the street along the canal to the bridge. He had no sooner arrived there than several Chinese soldiers, concealed behind the wall of Prince Su's palace, fired upon him. The sentry at the legation gate saw him hold up his hands, then heard a report and saw him fall. He was seen to partly raise himself, when several of the ruffian soldiers hurriedly ran out, picked him up, and carried him behind the corner of the wall and beyond, the reach of rescue. His fate was probably a hasty death at their hands, if, indeed, he was not already mortally wounded.

When I heard of this sad affair, an hour after its occurrence, I could scarcely believe that my friend who had welcomed me to China in 1885 had come to such a cruel end. He had not an enemy in the world, and was uniformly gentle and considerate. His fate, following so closely upon Baron von Ketteler's, the first day of our siege, cast a deep gloom over the entire community.

Promptly at 4 P.M. the Chinese soldiers opened fire upon all the legations from behind the surrounding houses; but, very fortunately for us, most of their bullets flew high and went entirely over the legation district and must have injured Chinese residents in Peking at a distance.

The British legation inside presented a scene of greatest confusion. Eatables and tinned stores of every description had been hastily dumped by coolies into all parts of the compound. Men, women, and children were busy for some hours trying to identify and collect the little stores they had brought or sent in, with the idea that a few days' provision would be all that would be necessary, as no one believed that Admiral Seymour, Colonel Wogack, and Captain McCalla would be longer than a week at most in relieving us.

Little did we imagine that many weeks of siege under shot,

shell, and rifle-fire must be endured, with absolutely no word from the outside world, before we, or at least such of us as survived, would again come forth.

Many had left their homes hurriedly, taking with them nothing but the clothes they wore. Having left my own house one week previous, and gone to the United States legation as a guest with my family, I had been requested not to bring in any supply of provisions, as it would alarm people, and it was hoped quiet would be restored in a few days.

When obliged by the Chinese ultimatum to leave Peking or, as we decided after Baron von Ketteler's murder, to take refuge in the British legation and await reinforcements, it was too late to visit my home outside of the foreign lines and remove anything from my storeroom.

Fortunately for my little family, Mr. H. G. Squiers, as I have mentioned, had laid in an abundant supply of rice, flour, and other stores, and he offered, if I would undertake to move all his stores safely to the British legation, to contribute to my needs. This I was only too glad to do; so, taking two of his servants and the only two of mine who, out of nine, had remained faithful, I worked from 9 A.M. until 4 P.M. removing Squiers' stores to the British legation.

I purchased, also, from one of the foreign stores within the lines of defense two dozen tins of condensed milk and four tins of baked beans, a very inadequate provision to feed six children and two adults for two months.

Many others were as poorly provided for as myself; but, providentially, within the region we had adopted as our lines of defense, were several large grain shops full of rice, wheat, and millet. Our carts were kept busy for several days hauling these supplies into the English legation, where they were placed in charge of a commissary officer and issued out as needed.

We thus had sufficient grain, not only for all the foreigners, but also for the two thousand odd refugees, coolies, and servants, who had, from one motive or another, cast their lot with us. From the grain shops, too, we brought in their millstones, and, as we had altogether over one hundred and fifty mules and horses, we started up a ten-mule-power mill, which ground out flour all day for the needs of the besieged.

Being occupied daily with the sanitary work and attendance on the sick, I was unable to keep much of a diary, so I instructed my son Robert, aged sixteen, to do so for me, and the following transcription of his diary gives the events of our daily life until the end of the siege.

June 21. Most of the Chinese coolies and many foreigners were set right at work filling sand-bags for fortifying all the weak places in the legation, while the women, with needle and thread and the few sewing machines inside the compound, manufactured the bags by the thousand. This was kept up until 20,000 to 25,000 sand-bags were made.

The Belgian legation and the Methodist mission were set fire to and completely burned. Tung Lu's troops kept up a desultory fusillade upon us all day, but scarcely any of the bullets took effect.

It was reported that Prince Ching's troops were firing on the Boxers, who were attacking the customs compound and Austrian legation. This report was afterward proved false. The French were driven from their barricade in the customs lane into the French legation compound.

The Chinese set fire to a native house just in the rear of Mr. Cockburn's house, hoping it would catch to the latter place. It was very near, and, as the wind was strong, was only prevented with the greatest difficulty from spreading into the legation. It was put out at last, after two hours' hard fighting. Some of the marines stationed as watchmen on the roof of the Cockburn house had seen Chinamen sneaking around with rags soaked in kerosene and had fired on them, but had not succeeded in preventing the fire being set.

The Austrians, Italians, Germans, and Japanese were forced by the heavy firing to leave their legations and come here. The

Americans also started, but were sent back. The Austrians and Italians were never able to retake their legations, but the Germans and Japanese returned very shortly to theirs. The Germans found a Boxer prisoner missing on their return on the 23d of June.

A fire was started just outside the north wall of the compound at 10 A.M., which was put out, or thought to have been put out; but it broke out again in the afternoon, this time burning a part of the Hanlin Library, adjoining the legation on the north. The conflagration was separated from the legation by only one narrow court, so one of the buildings in the court was pulled down to prevent its spreading. Thousands of wooden printing blocks were thrown into the fire to get rid of all combustible material in the immediate neighborhood. These blocks represent days of labor each, and were used in printing valuable (to the Chinese) books. Many valuable books also perished in the flames. At night a guard was placed in the Hanlin yuan, or garden, to watch the smoking remains, and, as this point is of greatest strategic importance, barricades will be erected here and the position maintained.

June 22. The customs compound and Austrian legation were burned, the Austrians remaining in the French legation to help them there. The back part of the Russo-Chinese bank compound was burned, also a house in the Japanese legation, which latter fire was soon subdued. A discharge of shrapnel from a gun on the city wall struck the gate house of the United States legation, and cut down the flag-pole, tearing a large hole in the roof, but hurting no one.

At 7 P.M. a house near the Hotel de Pein was burned. In this house two Boxers were captured. When seen, they threw down their swords and attempted to escape, but were caught and brought into the British legation to be locked up.

The fortifying operations are being pushed forward vigorously under the excellent management of Mr. F. D. Gamewell. He is the one man competent to take charge of affairs here, as the British, although in their own legation, and knowing that the place was to be the last place of refuge, had not done a stroke of work toward fortifying it, and seemed to be as helpless as children.

PORTION OF CHINA'S GREAT WALL
Showing one of the towers or forts, which are built at intervals throughout its entire length.

June 24. At ten minutes past midnight the Chinese began a furious fusillade from all quarters, and an alarm was rung from the bell-tower, notifying all of a general attack. But after about twenty minutes of prodigious noise, with almost no damage done, the firing ceased as suddenly as it had commenced, and the rest of the night was comparatively quiet. About 10 A.M. a fire was started outside and adjoining the south stables, which, after heroic exertions upon the part of nearly the entire garrison of men, women, and coolies, all of whom formed into line and passed hundreds of buckets of water from the two nearest wells to the scene of the fire, was subdued without our stables catching fire. With every one of these fires that was successfully put out, the danger from that source was lessened.

The German and American marines took possession of the city wall south of their respective legations, to prevent the Chinese from bringing their heavy guns too near and too directly able to bear upon the legations. Thrice they were driven back by the heavy fire, but they stuck to their task, and eventually obtained each a position on the wall—the Germans to the east, the Americans to the west, the two positions being about six hundred yards apart.

The second time they advanced, the Americans took the Colt machine gun with them, and, advancing almost to the Chinese barricade, killed several hundred Chinese. The third time, the Americans advanced several hundred yards and then retreated suddenly, as though panic-stricken. This brought the Chinese out from behind their barricades with a rush, when the Colt gun was again turned loose on them and killed sixty more.

After this the shelling got so hot that the position became absolutely untenable. A piece of shell struck the shoulder-piece of the Colt gun, and another shell, striking the wall, knocked down the bricks so thickly around the gun that Mitchell, the gunner, thought he might have to abandon it; but, hastily taking it apart, he managed to get it down the ramp, and brought it safely into the British legation.

The German officers claimed to have seen rockets to the southwest, which they thought to be signals from the relief force. Heavy cannonading was also heard, about 4 P.M., outside the city, which was thought to come from the troops, but both proved false hopes.

Corporal King, United States Marine Corps, was killed by a Chinese sniper in the Russo-Chinese bank. The United States barracks were set on fire, but fortunately the fire did not spread to the legation. Captain Halliday, Royal Navy Marine Corps, was severely wounded by a stray bullet. Thirteen men are in the hospital.

June 25. During the night one of the captured Boxers tried to escape, so in the morning they were both shot. There was about twenty minutes of hot firing about the same time as last night.

At 5 P.M. the Chinese put up a poster on the north bridge ordering the firing to stop, and to protect the ministers, stating also that they would send us a message. This message was never sent, however, and though the firing was stopped for a few hours, it soon started up again, and the whole thing was believed to be a fraud by which the Chinese wished to get some of the foreigners outside the legation to be killed.

The Americans and Germans again took their positions on the wall, and began building barricades in the face of the Chi-

ENTRANCE THROUGH GREAT
WALL INTO MONGOLIA —
ROTATING GATE
This great wall extends in massive
proportions over more than a thousand miles of plain and mountain. It
was built ages ago as a bar against
the incursions of the barbaric and
warlike tribes, who were destined
in time, despite this tremendous
obstacle, to overrun and acquire the
kingdom and place their own rulers
upon its throne.

nese gun. As the mutton began to get scarce, the first horse was killed. It was very good eating, and I doubt not that we have had some of that kind of beef before, in substitution for the genuine article. Three rockets, probably Chinese, were seen during the night.

June 26. The night entertainment — "fireworks" — came at 3 A.M., instead of midnight, as usual. Chinese troops were seen marching northwest, supposedly to convey the Empress to the summer palace. By this time the shells from the various guns close by us began to come nearer, several exploding in the compound. "Bombproof" cellars were therefore started in different parts of the compound, in which we might take refuge if the shells actually began to do damage. These "bomb-proofs" were trenches about six feet deep, covered with a roof of timbers, boards, and from two to four feet of earth or sandbags. These it was thought would furnish efficient protection against fragments of shell. Sergeant Fanning, United States Marine Corps, was killed by a sniper on the city wall.

June 27. Very heavy firing, mostly from the imperial city wall. A crowd of greenhorn Boxers started to attack the Americans on the wall from below. The Americans turned the Colt on them, killing about fifty, and the rest got away.

A Chinaman who arrived from near Tientsin reported Boxers very thick around there, and that three divisions of troops had left Tientsin June 24 to come to Peking, one coming north, one west, and one east.

June 28. No news of importance.

June 29. In the morning there was an attack made by the Chinese on the south stables, the weakest part of the whole legation compound. This was repulsed after a short fight, and about twenty British marines under Captain Strouts went out after the Chinese, killing a large number of them, and capturing their rifles with about six hundred rounds of ammunition. The guns were mostly Mauser rifles and carbines. They were distributed among the unarmed men of the legation. Captain Strouts was grazed in the neck by a bullet. Later fifty volunteers, under Captain Wray, went out to capture a gun near the Su Wang Fu that was making things unpleasant for the people there. They could not find it, however, and had to return.

By this time nearly all the Chinese houses near the United States legation had been burned in the various attempts to fire the legation, and in the ruins of these houses a number of Chinese snipers installed themselves, making it extremely dangerous for any one attempting to cross Legation street.

June 30. At night there was a very heavy thunderstorm, the first of the rainy season. Simultaneously with the thunder, the Chinese started a terrific fusillade from all quarters. The hideous noise, with the vivid flashes of lightning and the torrents of rain, produced an effect on the minds of all who witnessed it that they will probably never forget.

July 1. The Americans and Germans were forced by heavy shell-fire to leave the wall. Later in the day the Americans returned, but the Germans did not. The Chinese were quiet at night, there being hardly any firing at all. The reason for this was supposed to be temporary shortness of ammunition. At night a good many people believed they saw flashes from an electric searchlight, which was supposed to be with the troops at Tungchow. They claimed to have seen at first forty flashes, then an interval, followed by eight more. This they supposed to be some kind of a signal to us, but since it has all turned out to be heat lightning. Ed. Wagner, one of the customs men, was struck and killed in the French legation by a shell.

July 2. It rained at night, and no flashlights (?) were seen.

July 3. The Chinese on the wall had built up their barricade so high during the night that it almost overlooked our own (the two were only forty yards apart), and had they been able to build a little higher they might easily have fired right down on our men, so that it became a question of rushing the Chinese barricade or of leaving the wall. The former course was adopted. At 3 A.M., fifteen United States marines, fifteen Russian sailors, and twenty-five British marines, led by Captain John Myers, in the blackest part of the night, crept silently over the American barricade, and, dividing into two parties, each keeping close to either side of the wall battlements, advanced rapidly right up to the face of the Chinese barricade undiscovered. Arrived here, as agreed, they gave a tremendous yell, and swarmed over and around the barricade, yelling and firing volleys into the astonished Celestials, who, taken entirely by surprise by the yelling foreign devils, made very little resistance, and speedily fled to their second line of defense, some distance westward toward the Chien Men. Before starting, Captain Myers had briefly addressed his men, telling them the vital necessity of capturing the barricade. "Men," he said, "we must take that place at all costs or be driven off the wall! Once off the wall, the legations will lie at the mercy of the Chinese, and we, with all the women and children, will be butchered. This is our opportunity. I expect every man to do his duty. We cannot stop to pick up any who may be wounded, but must press on and accomplish the work, leaving the wounded until we return. If I fall, Sergeant Murphy of the British marines succeeds to command; if he falls Corporal Hunt of the American marines succeeds him. Now, when I give command, spring over the barricade, and follow me." He immediately gave the command: "Come on!" The sortie was most successful, the barricade was gained and held, but we lost two brave American boys, Privates Turner and Thomas. Captain Myers was badly wounded by a spear-thrust in his knee, and Corporal Gregory of the British marines was shot in the foot.

July 4. Independence day in America, but a day of red-hot fireworks for us. Chinese butchers on the outside trying hard to get in and murder us. Only celebration by Americans was a party given to the smaller children by Mrs. Squiers.

July 5. Mr. David Oliphant, one of the English legation students, was shot and mortally wounded, in the Hanlin Yuan. He died at 3, and was buried in our little graveyard at 7 P.M. His death threw a deep gloom over the whole legation, as he was a general favorite. Three attacks were made on us last night at 10 and 12, and 2.30 this morning. Cartridge ammunition of the enemy seems to be running low, as they are firing now more of the old muzzle-loading Yingalls, and fewer of the Mauser cartridges.

July 6. A sortie was made by the Japanese to try and capture a gun that was making havoc on their barricades in the Su Wang Fu. Too many Chinese houses, however, concealed the whereabouts of the gun, and after having three men wounded they were obliged to return unsuccessful. A shell fell in one of the rooms of Mr. Conger's house, doing considerable damage. Mrs. Conger had been in the room only a short time before.

A messenger was let down from the wall with ropes, to try and communicate our desperate situation to Tientsin. He was offered one thousand taels if he got safely through the enemy's lines with his dispatches. We have sent numerous runners out by the water-gate, and several over the wall, but none have ever returned. Doubtless they have been captured and killed.

During the day a number of three- and seven-pound solid iron shot have been thrown into our midst by guns located on the wall of the imperial, or yellow city, to the north of us. So far, beyond knocking a few holes in the buildings, they have done no harm. The powder they are using must be very inferior. One of the missiles passed through Lady MacDonald's dining room.

July 7. Two attacks were made on the French legation and were repulsed, the Chinese loss being small, as they retired rapidly. The Austrian commander, Captain von Thorneburg, was killed in one of these attacks, being shot through the heart.

We are now really eating the horse-meat. A number of people who were using it assured us it was very good, but our prejudices prevailed some time. First we tried the liver, fried with a small scrap of bacon, and were pleased to find it tasted just like beef-liver. Then we tried some of the meat curried, and now we are having excellent sausages of the meat, which helps the rice to be more palatable. We are allowed one pound of horse-meat per adult individual each day.

When the Russians came up the first time, they brought along with them sixty shells, leaving the gun in Tientsin to be brought up by the next force that came. As no other could get in, the ammunition was of no use. It was thought that if some kind of a cannon could be made, many of our shells might be utilized in destroying the Chinese barricades. So Mitchell, the United States gunner, started to work on two sections of a fire-engine pump. Meanwhile, two Chinese coolies found an old cannon, a muzzle-loader of about 1860, in a junkshop, and dragged it in. As this cannon fitted the shells it was used instead of the pump. It was mounted on a pair of wheels taken from the Italian ammunition truck. It has been nicknamed the "International." The gun itself was an old British one, mounted on an Italian carriage, and fired with Russian ammunition by an American gunner. Hence the nickname.

The ammunition for the Italian one-pound gun having run short, pewter vessels from the Chinese houses around were brought in, melted, and run into molds to make the shot for the gun. With these the used cartridges were reloaded, and, there being no primers for them, revolver cartridges were readily used instead. When tried in the bore they worked very well, though it was feared that the harder metal of which they were made would be ruinous to the rifling of the gun.

The Chinese broke two holes in the top of the imperial city wall and built a platform just over the water-gate, where it was expected they would mount guns the next night. At 10 P.M. they started a fusillade, which lasted for a few minutes, but the rest of the night was fairly quiet.

The French and Austrians claimed to have heard cannonading about ten kilometers (six miles) to the southeast. But this has also proved a false hope, and the general opinion is now that the relief has not started from Tientsin at all, though why, no one can say.

July 8. Sunday. The Chinese on the wall moved up their arms and opened fire on our barricade. The third shot they fired was badly aimed and struck their own barricade, carrying most of it away, when they were forced to retreat in a hurry. There was a fire at the Su Wang Fu of the main pavilion buildings, but it was not very serious. Two shells from a gun to the west struck the wall, and one the top of Mr. Coburn's house, showing that the Chinese are getting the range. The evening fusillade started at 9:45 and lasted about twenty minutes.

July 9. In the morning Mr. Squiers sent out a man into the city to see what was going on there. He returned in the afternoon reporting, first, that Hatamen has been closed for many days; second, that there are no Chinese troops in the southern city; third, that Rung Lu's troops are guarding the Chihaumen, but there are many Kansu men on the Hatamen streets and in the imperial city; fourth, that at the ssupailou (four arches) the shops are open and doing business as usual; fifth, that the Emperor and Empress Dowager are still in the city; sixth, that the Peking "Gazette" is published daily. The day was quiet except for occasional firing.

July 10. In the morning several of the Chinese shells came very close, breaking right over the tennis court, and making it unsafe for any one to cross.

July 11. A messenger sent out with a letter tried to get through the water-gate, but was immediately fired on by the Chinese sentries and forced to fly. He got in without being hurt.

The Chinese were extremely quiet all night, but the cause was not known until the next morning, when it was discovered that they had built two new big walls, one in the Hanlin Yuan, and another in the imperial carriage park.

July 12. The Chinese kept up a heavy cannonade all day, mostly from the guns on the imperial city wall, but did very little damage to us. A flag, white ground and black characters, was captured by the French in the morning, and in the afternoon Mitchell captured a big black one in the Hanlin Yuan. He got up on a Chinese barrier and wrested the flag from a Chinese soldier by pounding him with sandbags until he let go, while five or six volleys were fired at him. He secured the flag and got down without a scratch.

July 13. A Chinese prisoner taken by the French marines this morning states that the Emperor and Empress Dowager are still

Part of Author's Diary

in the palace here. Prince Tuan, Jung Lee and General Tung are in control of public affairs. Prince Ching takes no part in them. Many Boxers are still in the city. Their principal patron is Prince Tuan. In his palace they are registered, fed, and paid.

These Boxers are ridiculed by the soldiers because they dare not go under fire at the front, in spite of their pretensions to be bullet-proof.

General Tung's troops are facing us on the wall and along our lines on the south. Jung Lu's troops are behind the French legation. Several of them are killed or wounded every day. The prisoner declares that he was one of several coolies (hired at twenty-five cents a body) to carry off and bury the dead. There are about three thousand of Tung Fu Hsiang's troops in the city.

The Empress has forbidden the use of guns of large caliber against us, because of the harm they might do to her loyal people and their houses.

Direct attack having failed, and our rifles being better than theirs, it has been decided to starve us out. Two weeks ago news came that foreign troops from one hundred warships at Taku had captured the Taku forts, and occupied "East Taku," opposite Tangku railway station. Tientsin city was in a panic on this account.

Ammunition is being brought here from the Hunting park. Imperial edicts are issued as usual. Business is going on in the north part of the city, and market supplies are coming in. The four "chief banks" are closed. The soldiers believe that we have several thousand troops under arms here. The prisoner thought we had at least two thousand.

Of course, this information is not official, and there may be much that is not strictly accurate. It simply represents the gossip of the tea-shops and restaurants.

One reason the Chinese have for thinking we have so many men here is that a number of them are killed by their own bullets, which are aimed high and pass over our heads and drop among their own people. This shooting they attribute to our men, and so think we have a large force here.

Same date, 6.30 P.M. The Chinese exploded a mine under the French legation wall, destroying part of the wall and also part of their own fortifications. Four men were buried by the first explosion, one of whom was dug out, and another blown up again by a second explosion. Having done this, the Chinese made a desperate assault, but were beaten off after having killed three and wounded three French marines and lost about twenty of their number.

The minister's and first secretary's houses were fired, the minister destroying all his official papers himself, to prevent their falling into the hands of the Chinese.

Simultaneously with this attack came a tremendous fusillade from all sides, which lasted forty-five minutes, by far the longest we have had yet.

The Su Wang Fu was the scene of the hottest firing, and once it was thought it would have to be given up.

At the same time a body of Chinese, numbering about two hundred, charged down the wall street and got past the German legation without being stopped. When they got to the bridge, one of the United States marines was just coming down from the wall and saw them as they were coming up over the bridge. He gave the alarm to four men stationed in the barricade on the street, who fired about a dozen volleys on them, killing thirty of them. The natives then turned and fled; on the way back the Germans fired on them, driving them into the club tennis courts, where they killed eighteen more. The officer in command of the Chinese was shot by E. von Strauch, captain of the customs volunteers. In the fray two Germans were seriously, and two slightly, wounded. The Chinese kept up a desultory firing all night.

July 14. A large supply of wheat was brought over to the British legation from a grain store near the south bridge, and distributed in several storerooms throughout the compound. This was done as there had been some burning near there, and it was feared it would be destroyed. A messenger sent out by Mr. Tewksbury on the 10th instant returned, bringing a message supposed to have been written by Prince Ching. It was soon known to be an invitation to leave the legations and go to the tsung-li-yamen for protection, though the full translation was not put upon the bulletin board till the next day.

July 15. The following bulletin was posted at 1 P.M.:

A messenger sent out on July 10 by Mr. Tewksbury, with a letter for the troops, returned yesterday. He is the gate-keeper at the Nan Vang (south cathedral) and a Roman Catholic. He says he was arrested outside the Hatamen and taken to the Wofursu (temple?), his letter was taken from him, and he was beaten with eighty blows. He was then taken to Jung Lu's headquarters in the imperial city. Here he found a man named Yu who formerly knew him as gatekeeper. He was there given a letter, purporting to be written by Prince Ching and others, addressed to the British minister, and told that men would wait at the water-gate to-night for an answer. A translation of the letter is annexed:

"For the last ten days the soldiers and militia have been fighting, and there has been no communication between us, to our great anxiety. Some time ago we hung up a board (referring to June 25) expressing our intentions, but no answer has been received, and, contrary to expectation, the foreign soldiers made renewed attacks, causing alarm and suspicion among people and soldiers.

"Yesterday the troops captured a convert named Chin Ssu Hai, and learned from him that the foreign ministers were all well, which caused us great satisfaction. But it is the unexpected that happens — the reinforcements of foreign troops were ever so long ago stopped and turned back by the Boxers, and if, in accordance with the previous agreement, we were to guard your excellencies out of the city, there are so many Boxers on the Tientsin-Taku road that we should be very apprehensive of misadventure.

[ 64 ]

"We now request your excellencies to first take your families and the various members of your staff, and leave your legations in detachments. You should select trustworthy officers to give close and strict protection, and you should temporarily reside in the. tsung-li-yamen, pending future arrangements for your return home in order to preserve friendly relations intact from beginning to end. But at the time of leaving the legations there must on no account whatever be any single armed foreign soldier, in order to prevent doubt and fear on the part of the troops and people, leading to untoward incidents.

"If your excellency is willing to show this confidence, we beg you to communicate with all the foreign ministers in Peking, to-morrow at noon being the limit of time, and to let the original messenger deliver your reply, in order that we may settle in advance the day for leaving the legations. This is the single way of preserving relations that we have been able to devise in the face of innumerable difficulties. If no reply is received by the hour fixed, even our affection will not enable us to help you. Compliments.

PRINCE CHING AND OTHERS."
"6th moon, 18th day [July 13, 1900]."

A reply has been sent to-day declining, on the part of the foreign representatives, the invitation to proceed to the tsung-li-yamen, and pointing out that no attacks have been made by our troops, who are only defending the lives and property of foreigners against the attacks of Chinese government troops. The reply concludes with a statement that if the Chinese government wishes to negotiate, they should send a responsible official with a white flag.

CLAUDE M. MACDONALD.

This message is thought by everyone to be a rank fraud. It is supposed to come not from Prince Ching, but from the leader of the Kansu troops, and is probably intended to lure some of the foreigners outside the legation and then to shoot them.

Same date, 3 P.M. Twenty Russians and four Americans made an attack on a house to the west of the Russian legation, where there were about sixty Chinese snipers. On arriving at the wall they found there was no way to get into the yard. So each man took a brick, and, at a given signal, heaved them all together into the yard, shouting and reviling the Chinamen.

Alarmed by this they fled, and the men took the building without a shot being fired on either side. At this time the Chinese at other points started up a brisk fire, lasting about ten minutes.

July 16, 7 A.M. While on a tour of inspection in the Su Wang Fu, in company with Dr. Morrison and Colonel Shiba, Captain B. M. Strouts, R.M.L.I., was shot and mortally wounded by a sniper. Dr. Morrison was shot in the leg, though not seriously. Captain Strouts died at 11 A.M. and was buried at 6 P.M. yesterday. One of the United States marines, Private Fisher, was killed the same day.

It is indeed a pitiable plight that we are in now. Neither the Americans nor the British have any leader. Captain Meyers is disabled by the spear wound he received in the sortie of July 3. Captain Strouts is dead; Captain Halliday, the only other able British captain, is crippled by a wound received three weeks ago. Sir Claude MacDonald, though he assumes charge, is no man for the situation, and the French and Germans deny his authority.

Same date, 5 P.M. The messenger sent yesterday returned with four others, who waited for him at the bridge. He brought a letter from Jung Lu to Sir Claude MacDonald, and a telegram from Washington to Mr. Conger. The letter to Sir Claude contained nothing of any importance. The telegram, Mr. Conger recognized as being in the State Department cipher, but could not determine its meaning, as it had evidently been tampered with in some way by the Chinese. So the messenger was sent back with a request that the full original telegram be sent.

July 17. The messenger returned again bringing a telegram

VIEW FROM THE WALL OF PEKING SHOWING SCENE OF THE BLOCKADE AND
OTHER POINTS OF SPECIAL INTEREST
1. The prominent building at this point is the British Legation, practically the headquarters
of the defense.
2. This high wall, extending the entire length of the picture, marks the boundary of the
"For-bidden City"; at the point indicated, the Krupp guns, mentioned in the narrative, were
mount-ed, giving them a sweeping range of Legation street.
3. The residence of the author after the siege, his own property having been so badly dam-
aged by the mob as to make it untenantable.
4. The roof of the American Legation (in another picture is shown a view of the Legation
itself).
5. The Russian Legation, another of the most important points in the foreign field of defense.
6. Bridge over the canal at Legation street. The foul and stagnant water in the canal and the
filth in its bed are plainly shown.
7. The roofs of the Emperor's palace and "Forbidden City" and other portions of some of the
buildings appear above the wall that surrounds it. It will be noticed that, while strictly barred
out from the "Forbidden City" and the palace of the Emperor, the foreign legations were nevertheless within a comparatively short distance.
8. The top of what is known as the "Coal Hill," in the Imperial grounds of the "Forbidden
City," shows over the top of the wall. This hill is a vast supply of coal, which has been ac-
cumulating for hundreds of years. It is entirely without shelter, and there seems to be no
authentic history to account for its inception, nor any special reason for its continuance;
but here, in the most sacred place in the Chinese kingdom, right in the magnificent palace
grounds of the Emperor, this ugly, unsightly pile of coal, covering several acres in extent and
rising, as can be seen by the picture, to a very considerable height, washed by the rains and
seamed by the upheavals of the frosts of winter, continues to exist, as it has done from time
immemorial.

MAIN STREET OF PEKING FROM THE
CITY WALL

This shows the main street of Peking-its
"Market street," as Philadelphians might
say, or its "Strand," from the English point
of view. Although a main street it is scarcely
better than a country road, and busy trading seems to be going on in the foreground
in the open air. Here and there a sign
indicates that business is conducted within,
and that unavoidalbe feature of a Chinese
city, the open pool of stagnant water, is in
evidence.

MEMORIAL ARCHES

It is doubtful if we should have been able to
learn so much of the "Forbidden City" and
of the beautiful and remarkable things to be
seen in the Palace grounds had it not been
for this Siege. These are most beautiful from
a Chinese point of view, the architecture dat-
ing back for many ages. These arches are
built of immense blocks of stone, beautifully
fitted and arranged.

A temple in the Summer Palace grounds

CHINESE STATESMEN
A group of Chinese officials of the highest
class; in Peking, previous to the Siege.

A GROUP OF PROMINENT CHINESE OFFICIALS
These men are connected with the Tsung-li-yamen.

A group in front of the American Legation (L-R): Hsu Yung I, Beheaded Aug. 9, 1900; Wang Wen Shao; Chao Shu Chiao, Boxer Chief; Conger, U.S. Minister; Yu Keng, Minister to Paris

BRIDGE AT WAN SHOA SHAN, NEAR PEKING
That the Chinese appreciate the picturesque, both in situation and in architecture, is shown in this picture.

HOUSE BOATS
Used for interior travel in Chinese rivers. Families pass their entire existence on these boats. Some are fitted very comfortably

BALED TEA READY FOR SHIPMENT TO RUSSIA

Some idea of the great quantities of tea produced, and of the method of packing, may be gathered from this picture.

BUIDING BARRICADES IN GERMAN LEGATION

Without the barricades the defense would never have been successful. Some very hard fighting was done in the vicinity of this barricade. The lower portion was built of brick, with sand-bags on top and loop-holes left for the purpose of rifle firing.

APPROACH TO HATAMEN GATE IN WALL DESTROYED BY THE RUSSIANS

Elsewhere in this work is presented a view of the top of this wall, indicating its great width. This view shows its height and form. To the left is the encircling canal, with its stagnant water and accumulations of filth; under a corner of the wall near the bend of the canal may be seen a caravan. A block house or for-tification is shown on top of the wall. At the right the larger building upon the top of the wall indicates where one of the city gates is placed. The foundation of the wall is of great blocks of hewn stone, above which are tiers of sun-dried brick.

VIEW IN LEGATION STREET

The entrance to French legation is on the left. The lions shown on either side of the entrance are such as can be found nowhere outside of China. The street is in somewhat better condition, since it is presumably under foreign control, or at least is modified by foreign influences.

I—4

On the great wall, Kun Ming Hu

Chinese gentleman entertaining a friend with an opium pipe

GENERAL SUNG CHING
Commander-in-Chief, who fought the battle of Tientsin against the allied international armies.

GENERAL MA YU KUN
Major-General under Sung Ching also engaged in the battle of Tientsin with the allied international armies.

STREET VENDERS OF TIENTSIN
A vast amount of business is transacted by these merchants, whose stock in trade is of the smallest, and whose transactions are so insignificant as to be incredible according to western ideas.

A MONGOLIAN LLAMA
Great learning is possessed, according to the Chinese standard, by these priests. The young student or candidate on the left is receiving instruction.

SIKH POLICEMAN
The two Oriental types, East Indian and Chinese, are plainly shown in this picture. The policeman looms up almost like a giant in the midst of his Celestial neighbors.

**A WOMAN OF NORTH CHINA**
It is not easy to obtain pictures of the women of the upper classes of China. The beautiful cape with the elaborate embroidery, the little feet mounted upon pedestals, and that sign of high nobility, the long finger nails, shown by nail protectors on the third and fourth fingers of the left hand, are evidences that this woman is of China's "four hundred."

**A PEKING BELLE**
Perhaps, after looking at this picture, there will not be so much wonder that occasionally a Caucasian selects a Chinese girl for a wife. That there are very attractive Chinese girls this picture evidences. The clothing, the ornaments, and the surroundings are all typical.

Native wheelbarrow — Tientsin

Taoist Temple of ten thousand gods in Nanking

VOLUNTEERS OF THE RUSSO-CHINESE
BANK
This picture was not taken during the Siege,
as these gentlemen had something else to
do during that time. It was not even taken
after the Siege, and it is a question whether
they will ever be as happy and free from
care again. One has passed away forever, the
gentleman in the chair to the right, who was
killed in an engagement with the Boxers. After hard fighting, in which a number were
killed, the Boxers carried away his body.

GORDON HALL
In the cellar of this building all the women
and children remained during the shelling
of Tientsin by the Chinese troops. It is one of
the most beautiful and attractive buildings
in Tientisin, and in strange contrast with its
Chinese surroundings.

UNITED STATES LEGATION
Dr. Coltman's rooms were at the left, Minister Conger's the right. The yard or "compound" is paved, with openings for the trees
and vegetation. The most attractive part of
the house, as is the case with nearly all Chinese houses, is that which looks upon the
compound instead of the street.

TEA CARAVAN RESTING OUTSIDE
OF CITY WALL
One might imagine this picture to illustrate
a scene in Bible times, in Palestine or Egypt;
but time does not make any changes in China; nothing changes there, save through the
influence of outside aggression. Here is a caravan from the interior of Asia, halted outside
the city wall for entrance in the morning. The
burdens have been taken from the camels and
the beasts have settled for rest.

Inside one of the United States Legation rooms

The United States Legation Staff (L-R): Mr. F. D. Cheshire, Interpreter; Mr. H. G. Squiers, Second Secretary; Mr. E. H. Conger, Minister; Mr. W. E. Bainbridge, First Secretary.

FAMILY OF THE AUTHOR
All of the persons in this group, with the exception of the author's father standing in the center, and his mother at the left, suffered in the Siege.

Chinese barber and his outfit

SIR ROBERT HART
And members of the Customs Staff and their families, with one or two others, who lived together in the house immediately behind the group during the siege.

CUSTOMS VOLUNTEERS
Who, throughout the siege, fought in defense of the legations. This little band did excellent service. Brave, cool and deliberate, they made themselves felt wherever their services were called for.

CHINESE LITTER
A typical method of Chinese conveyance. The litter is supported by poles to the backs of two animals, one in front, the other behind; in it the traveler can make himself comfortable. Beyond are the massive tombs of the Ming Dynasty, the famous arches of which are shown elsewhere.

PASSENGER WHEELBARROW
This picture shows the common method of transportation in vogue in the Chinese cities of today; but with the opening of China to western influences the modern electric car will doubtless supersede this conveyance, and, like many other picturesque but antiquated features of the country, it will be relegated to the past.

Russian Minister and Staff of Legation and their families

IMPERIAL PAVILION
The Hall of Classics, in the Forbidden City,
Peking— a beautiful building

Madame Chamot, the heroine of the siege

A Chinese cart

Group of natives, Su Chan Gardens

Typical Peking beggars

MARQUIS TSENG'S DAUGHTER AND
HER HUSBAND
In their wedding finery. The familiar gera-
nium between shows that the Chinese have
our flowers.

Two singing girls of Peking

HERBERT G. SQUIERS
First Secretary, United States Legation, Peking

from Wu Ting Fang, the Chinese minister at Washington, enclosing one from the Secretary of State. This read: "Communicate tidings to bearer." To this the minister sent in reply: "One month in the British legation under shot and shell. Will all be massacred unless help comes soon."

One of Jung Lu's soldiers came in the morning and gave himself up at the German legation, and asked for some medicine for a wound in the ear. He said that Jung Lu had ordered the soldiers to stop firing, but to hold their positions, and that he was very desirous that the foreigners should be protected.

Not a shot has been fired since early morning. This is probably due to a fear that the foreign troops are near, and the government wishes to protect itself by saying they were unable to control the Boxers and the Kansu soldiers. Several other Chinese soldiers gave themselves up as prisoners at the different legations, though with what purpose no one can say.

July 18. As Jung Lu had expressed a willingness to assist the foreigners, a messenger was sent to him requesting that supplies of fresh vegetables, eggs, meat, etc., might be sent to the legation for the women and children. This was promised, and watermelons and peaches have already been sent to the Japanese in the Su Wang Fu and to the Americans on the wall. The soldiers on the wall go on each other's barriers and chat in the most friendly manner. There are great numbers of Boxers in the city, especially in the south city, but the troops are no longer in league with these.

A messenger sent out by the Japanese minister on the 30th ult. returned to-day from Tientsin, bringing word that a mixed force of 33,300 would start from there for the relief of Peking about the 20th inst. The force is to consist of 24,000 Japanese, 4,000 Russian, 2,000 British, 1,500 American, 1,500 French, and 300 German troops.

He reports that he left by the Ch'ihuamen (east gate) on June 30, proceeding to Tientsin by boat. He arrived at Tientsin on July 5, but was unable to enter the city, as it was surrounded by Chinese troops. He walked round the city gates, and found a force of Chinese, under General Chang, posted north of the railway station, cannonading a force of Japanese holding the ground south of the station.

On July 9 General Chang was defeated, and he (the messenger) managed to get through the Japanese lines on July 12, and delivered the Japanese minister's letter to the Japanese consul.

While in Tientsin he gleaned the following news: That General Nieh was dead, that all the missionaries in Tientsin and outlying stations had left for home, and that the Taku forts were taken without difficulty by the foreigners on June 17. On July 14 the foreign troops took the native city of Tientsin, after a two days' attack. On July 15 the messenger left Tientsin for Peking, being escorted by the Japanese to the "second bridge." He returned to Peking by road.

Among other things he mentioned was that the Tunchou taotai had been lodged in the board of punishments, and that prior to his own arrival in Tientsin. No news of Peking had reached that place since about the end of June.

We look for the troops about the 30th inst., if they have no fighting to do on the way. This explains why the government is so anxious to have peace in the capital at present. They are awaiting the issue of a contest between the relief force and the Chinese troops between here and Tientsin.

If our troops are victorious, as of course they will be, unless outnumbered overwhelmingly, the government will say they have done all in their power to stop the fighting, but have not been able to control their troops until now. If our troops are defeated they will turn on us and slaughter us. In the meantime we have a resting spell of a few days.

Bulletin: Précis of further correspondence between the British minister and "Prince Ching and others."

On July 16 the Chinese sent a reply to Sir Claude's letter of the 15th, in which they explain that the reason for suggesting the removal of the legation staffs to the tsung-li-yamen was that the Chinese government could afford more efficient protection to them if concentrated there than if scattered, as at present. As the foreign ministers, however, do not agree, the Chinese will, as in duty bound, do their utmost to protect the legations where they are. They will bring reinforcements, and continue their efforts to prevent the Boxers from firing, and they trust the foreign ministers on their part will restrain their troops also from firing.

July 17, A.M. Sir Claude replied to the effect that the foreign troops had all along acted entirely in self-defense and would continue to do so. But the Chinese must understand that previous events had led to a want of confidence, and that if barricades were erected or troops moved in the vicinity of the legations, the foreign guards would be obliged to fire on them.

July 17 P.M. The Chinese replied, reviewing the situation and ascribing the present hostilities to the attacks previously made by the legation guards. They noted with satisfaction that a cessation of firing is agreed to on both sides, but suggest that as foreign soldiers here have been firing from the city wall east of the Chien Men, they should be removed from that position.

July 18 (noon). Sir Claude replied with a review of the situation from the foreign point of view. On June 19 the yamen had given the legations notice to quit Peking, and the foreign representatives had replied, pointing out that there were no facilities of transportation. The yamen had then replied, extending the time; but, in spite of this, fire was opened on the legations on the following day, and they had been under constant fire from Chinese government troops ever since, a condition of things unparalleled in the world's history. He alluded to the incident of the board displayed on June 25, the free moving of troops during the cessation of hostilities thus caused, and the renewed attacks made after the completion of the preparations thus facilitated. He hoped that mutual confidence would gradually be restored, but meanwhile he again pointed out that cessation of hostile preparations, as well as of actual firing, was necessary on the part of the Chinese forces to secure that the foreign troops should cease shooting. As for the suggestion that the foreign troops should leave the city wall, it was impossible to accede to it, because a great part of the attacks on the legation had been made from the wall. He concluded by suggesting that sellers of fruit or ice should be allowed to come in.

In a letter addressed the same day to Jung Lu, the substance of Sir Claude's previous letters was repeated, and a suggestion was made that communications would be facilitated if a responsible official were sent to the legation. In response to this suggestion, a yamen secretary arrived this afternoon with a card from Jung Lu. He had no special message, but promised to see whether Peking "Gazettes" could be procured and a market established for ice, fruit, eggs, etc., and also to ascertain whether telegrams could be transmitted on behalf of the foreign ministers to their governments. He mentioned that telegraphic communication was interrupted. He expressed the concern of the Chinese government at the deeds of the Boxers, who had caused the whole difficulty between China and the foreign powers.

July 19. A very quiet day. No firing on either side. About two hundred and fifty eggs and a few vegetables were brought in by Chinese soldiers for sale. The yamen sent another message asking that the ministers leave here for Tientsin.

July 20. Several copies of the Peking "Gazette" of the past month were procured from the Chinese. Translations of a number of edicts contained therein are given in another chapter. The ministers replied to the yamen's request of yesterday, saying that, as the Boxers were so numerous outside the city, they would not dare to trust themselves on the road. Four cart-loads of watermelons and vegetables were sent to the ministers by the yamen as a sign of good feeling (?). No firing all day, except for a few shots fired by Boxers in the south city against our men on the wall.

July 24. Mr. Narahara, second secretary of the Japanese legation, died in the early morning, of lockjaw from a wound.

Same date, 7 P.M. The following was received from Colonel Shiba: "A Chinaman who came to our barricade this afternoon says that on the 17th of this month Yangtsun was occupied by the foreign troops, and on the 19th a battle took place around the same place. About one hundred and fifty wounded of Tung Fu Hsiang's troops have just been brought to Peking; the foreign troops were about forty li this side of Yangtsun when the wounded men started."

July 26. Colonel Shiba reports: "A Chinaman states that about 11 o'clock on the 24th instant the Chinese troops under General Chang were attacked by foreign troops thirty li south of Hoshiwu (half-way between Tientsin and here by road) and driven back at midnight to the latter place. At 10 A.M. yesterday Hoshiwu was attacked, and the Chinese troops driven back with heavy loss to ten li north of the latter place. The force of 4,800 men who came from the west with nine guns left Peking at 6 o'clock yesterday morning for Hoshiwu."

Since the beginning of the truce, on July 18, the soldiers of Jung Lu have observed the truce and refrained from firing; but those fronting us on the north wall and on the west of the legation have started sniping again. The latter are Tung Fu Hsiang's troops.

July 25. Chin Tsu-hsi, a messenger who left our lines eight days ago carrying an official letter to Jung Lu, returned to-day. He says that he delivered the letter at Jung Lu's headquarters, and was locked up there seven days. Jung Lu goes to court every day. The Emperor and Empress Dowager are still in the city. Boxers patrol the streets in small bands.

Four days ago a ragged, dirty foreigner, hatless and coatless, of general disreputable appearance, was captured by Tung Fu Hsiang's men and brought to Jung Lu. He was of medium height, blonde mustache and beard, and spoke Chinese. (This referred to a Swede named Nestergaard, who, on some slight offense, left the legation and went over to the Chinese.) He said he went out to find food. Meanwhile Boxers assembled around Jung Lu's house, and demanded the foreigner, but Jung Lu sent him off under guard to the yamen of the Shun Tien Fu for safe keeping.

A messenger sent out on July 4 to go to Tientsin with our letter returned to-day, bringing the following note from the British consul at Tientsin:

> Your letter of July 4 received. There are now 24,000 troops landed and 10,000 here. General Gaselee expected at Taku to-morrow. Russian troops are at Peitsang. Tientsin city is under foreign government, and Boxer power here is exploded. There are plenty of troops on the way if you can keep yourselves in food. Almost all ladies have left Tientsin.
>
> (Signed) W. R. CARLES.
> Dated July 22.

(The letter of July 4 gave details of the siege up to that date, numbers of killed and wounded, and stated that Chinese troops had fired into the legation quarter continuously since June 20, and that we were hard pressed.)

This answer of the British consul aroused great indignation among all the besieged. It had been impossible up to that time to get any word from the outside world, though many messengers were sent out, and then when one did succeed in getting through the Chinese lines, to receive a letter (and that from an official, too) which gave no information of any attempt to relieve us!

Following is the story of the runner's trip to Tientsin and back: Lin Wu Yuan, sixteen years old, a messenger, native of Shantung, living in Peking, arrived this morning, from Tientsin. He left Peking with letters on the night of July 4, disguised as a beggar. He was let down over the wall by a rope, crept along the moat to the Chien Men, slept under the gate, and in the morning walked to the Yungting Men, passed through, and went to Machiapu station without being molested.

Hearing nothing there, he went to Tungchow and worked his way along the main road to Tientsin. At a village near Hoshiwu he was stopped by the villagers and made to work eight days. He reached Tientsin July 18, first met Russian, then Japanese, and on July 21 met the British troops at Peiving Men, the entrance through the defense wall, half a mile from Tientsin city, on the Peking road.

He delivered his letter to a foreigner in citizen dress, who spoke Chinese. On July 22 he was taken to the British consulate; there the consul gave him a letter. He was then sent to the foreign outpost at Hungch'iao (Red Bridge over the Paotingfu river, a half mile west of Tientsin city).

On July 23 he left Hungch'iao, and soon met the Chinese troops. That night he slept at Yangtsun in a locomotive boiler near the bridge. The bridge there was not destroyed. That day he saw only Chinese infantry, the main body of which was at Peitsang; he saw no Boxers. The night of July 24 he slept near Hoshiwu; saw few soldiers and no Boxers. The night of July 25 he slept at Mat'ou. That day he saw a few parties of Boxers in villages, but none on the road.

At Mat'ou and elsewhere he saw that the river was in high flood; few boats moving, but many moored to the banks. On July 26 had no adventures; he spent the night at Yuchiawei, twenty li from Peking.

On July 27 he reached the Sha Kuo gate, the east gate of the south city, at 10 A.M. He found the roads good; telegraph poles and wire along the river all gone; railway torn up everywhere, rails buried, or used for making Boxer swords.

He was not stopped at the gate, though there were many Boxers and Tung Fu Hsiang's men there. He made his way without trouble to the Hatamen, which he found closed, and to the water-gate, which was too closely guarded to pass by day. The man slept last night near the Chien Men, crawled along the moat, and entered the water-gate without challenge before daylight this morning.

He said the high road to Tientsin is in good condition. Crops everywhere look well. Villagers are attending to their farms, but there is a Boxer organization in every village. When he left Tientsin, the foreign troops had not advanced beyond the defense wall, San Ko Hin Sin's "Folly," built by that general against the British and French in 1860 but never defended (hence the name "folly") surrounding Tientsin city at a distance of one-half to one mile. All the yamens in Tientsin are occupied by foreign troops, chiefly Japanese. All Boxers have left the front at Tientsin because badly punished in the battle, so the Chinese soldiers despise them. Chinese army was concentrating on Peitsang, eight miles northwest of Tientsin. The messenger had a dollar in his pocket when he met the foreign pickets at Tientsin, and they relieved him of it, "lest he might lose it"!

Colonel Shiba's informant gives the following dates of battles:

Battle at Tsaitsun, July 24, 1 to 12 P.M.

Battle at Hoshiwu, July 25, 10 A.M. to 3 P.M.

Battle at Auping, July 26, 6 to 9 P.M.

Chinese troops retired to Mat'ou on the 27th inst.

July 29. Reports from various sources, etc.: Foreign troops advance on the 26th from Auping toward Mat'ou, from 3 A.M. to 12 M., and were driven back to Auping by the Chinese at daylight on the 27th.

Foreign troops of three nationalities at Auping. Chinese ammunition short; southern rice boats in the hands of the foreign army. Russian troops are advancing toward Kalgan (from a man from Changpingchou, eighteen miles south of the Great Wall).

July 29 P.M. Reported Yangtsun completely destroyed by foreign troops two or three days ago, and foreign army in steady advance. The Empress Dowager desires Tung Fu Hsiang and Jung Lu to send her with an army to Hsianfu, the capital of Shansi. They do not consent, and suggest Li Ping Heng to help conquer us. He is ordered up, has arrived, and is now attacking the Peit'ang. During the night a strong barricade was built on the north bridge; two hundred Boxers took up a position on it and commenced firing.

July 30, 10 A.M. The Chinese army messenger left Changchiawan at 8 o'clock yesterday evening. He reports desultory fighting from 3 A.M. to 8 P.M. yesterday. Many Chinese were killed. The foreign army advanced to Mat'ou yesterday at 8 A.M. Chinese retreated on Changchiawan. They have about 10,000 men. Three cannon have been taken from the Chien Men to the front. Fighting at Peit'ang is continued by Boxers. The firing from the north bridge is by a company of two hundred Boxers having only thirteen rifles. The Empress has three hundred carts and Tung Fu Hsiang one hundred, ready to start west; the date is a secret. Tung's fourth son, with five hundred men, has reached Lianghsiang on the way west. (This news was brought in by a soldier of Tung Fu Hsiang's body-guard, who brings us regularly the report of the army messenger.)

Same date, 7:30 P.M. Yesterday morning Mr. Sugi sent two outside coolies to Tungchow to inquire in regard to the foreign army, etc. They returned this evening. They report that men in Tungchow affirm that the foreign army had fought the Chinese yesterday just south of Mat'ou. They also report having seen a man from Chiachiatuan (eight miles east of Tungchow) who says foreign troops have come to relieve the Catholics there, and are distant but a mile or so from the intrenchments, letters having already been exchanged.

The Peking gates, except the Chihua Men and the Pingtzu Men, are ready to be closed, with stone and sand-bags at their sides. Many Boxers have been killed at the Peit'ang; twelve regiments of General Ma's troops are to go to Changchiawan.

We have given each of these coolies a small letter to the commander of the troops and offered a reward for a return to-morrow night with an answer. The troops must be pretty near us, and we may hope to see them in two days.

July 31, 11 A.M. The regular Chinese army courier arrived from the field of battle this morning at 4:30. He reports, in the hearing of one of Tung Fu Hsiang's body-guard, the same man who has brought us the reports of the movements of the foreign army from Yangtsun, the foreign army advanced from Mat'ou, fighting from 8 P.M. on the 29th, and arrived at Changchiawan at 5 P.M. yesterday. The Chinese army is five miles south of Tungchow.

August 1. The following letter received to-day by Colonel Shiba, dated Tientsin, the 26th ult.:

"Your letter of the 22d received. Departure of troops from Tientsin delayed by difficulties of transportation, but advance will be made in two or three days. Will write again as soon as estimated date of arrival at Peking is fixed."

A somewhat mangled but authentic telegram has been received from London. The telegram is undated, but was sent off probably between the 21st and 24th ult. It refers to a letter written by the Japanese minister about June 29, and to a telegram from the United States minister, dated July 18, from which it may be inferred that the state of affairs here on the latter date was everywhere known. It also says that the Chinese troops, after severe fighting, were finally routed from Tientsin on the 15th ult., and that arrangements for our relief were being hastened. It further asks if the Chinese government is protecting us and supplying provisions, etc.!

Very few provisions have been sent in to-day. A desultory firing has been kept up all the time from the north bridge and the Mongol market. The messenger, who has been bringing in the previous rumors of the progress of the troops, said that they had been driven back from Changchiawan to Auping. As the letter from Tientsin has proved him an arrant liar, in future no more attention will be paid to his stories. It is a great disappointment, after being told that the relief were within two days of us, to hear that they have not yet started and have not yet fixed a date for starting.

The messenger's story has been well arranged all along, and

has agreed very well with the letter received by the Japanese minister on July 18. As we have had no later information (the British consul's letter gave none) as to the movements of the army, we have believed just what the Chinaman told us, and as long as he was getting paid for it he would give us any kind of rumors.

August 2. Extracts from various letters received from Tientsin:

### Mr. E. B. Drew to Sir Robert Hart, July 28.

"Yours of 21st wired home. Keep heart; aid coming early. Troops pouring in. Enemy is at Peits'ang. Japs and Russians in his front. Very little rain. Yangtzu valley agitated. Lu and Chang trying to keep order. Li Hung Chang at Shanghai; doubtful if he is coming to Chihli. Tientsin is governed by a joint foreign commission. Manchuria rising against foreigners. Russians, hands full there. Newchwang much disturbed. Germany and America each sending 15,000 men, Italy 5,000 — Canton, west river. Ichang threatening. Earnestly hope rescue of you all."

### Mr. E. K. Lowry to Mrs. Lowry, July 30.

"Bearer arrived last Friday evening, with news from Peking. . . . The 9th and 14th regiments, United States, already at Tientsin; 6th cavalry at Taku on its way up. There was fighting at Piets'ang this morning. Everything quiet here now. Word came to-day that the Boxers are killing Christians at Tsunhua, Shanhaikuan, and many other places. Russians and imperial troops have fought at Chinhau. Tientsin is full of foreign soldiers and more are coming all the time. Railroad open between here and Tangku. Many ladies and children were taken to the United States by the transport Logan. All property at Peitaiho has been destroyed."

### Consul Ragsdale to Mr. Conger, July 28.

"Had lost all hope of ever seeing you again. Prospect now brighter. We had thirty days' shelling here, nine days' siege — thought that bad enough. Scarcely a house escaped damage. Excitement at home intense, of course. Our prayers and hope are for your speedy rescue. Advance of troops to-morrow probable."

From J. S. Mallory, Lieutenant-colonel 41st U.S. Infantry.
"A relief column of 10,000 is on the point of starting for Peking; more to follow. God grant they may be in time."

Colonel Warren to Captain Myers.
"Have been trying to reach you ever since June 21. Relieved the foreign settlement June 23. Seymour, June 24. Captured east arsenal June 26; captured west arsenal July 10; captured Tientsin city July 14. Will advance in two days. Column 10,000 strong, — English, American and Japanese; 40,000 more following in a few days. Hold on by all means. First column will support you and divert enemy from you. There will be eight regiments of United States infantry, three of cavalry and two batteries of artillery; also five hundred marines. Infantry will be in the first column. Enemy strongly intrenched seventeen miles north of here (Yangt-sun), and at two points farther on."

The Customs volunteers took up a new position on the Mongol market, on the southwest of the British legation.

LI HUNG CHANG
China's greatest Viceroy

August 3. Another message was received from the yamen requesting us to leave the legation and go to Tientsin. The Chinese are extremely anxious to get us out of Peking, as they think that with us out of the way the armies will have no particular reason to come to Peking and will be content to settle up matters at Tientsin.

August 4. A great deal of firing all night. Two Russians were wounded while building a barricade, one of whom died during the night.

August 6. A sharp fusillade at 1 A.M., otherwise a quiet day. The firing, which throughout the first few days after the truce amounted only to a few scattering shots, has come to be nearly as hot as before the truce, and attacks are being made again every night.

August 8. The ministers received an official message from the tsung-li-yamen saying: "By an imperial edict dated August 7, full power has been granted to Li Hung Chang to discuss and arrange all matters by telegraph with the foreign offices of all the powers."

Colonel Shiba reported that a Chinese outside coolie came in to say that all the troops in Peking, with the exception of five battalions of Jung Lu's, have been, or are going to be, dispatched in great haste to meet the foreign troops; he does not know where the latter are. He adds that another 50,000 foreign troops have been landed at Taku.

August 9. Sniper firing all day from Tung Fu Hsiang's troops, especially at the customs position in the Mongol market. The latter were several times silenced by volleys from the Nordenfeldt machine gun mounted on a parapet built against the west wall of the legation. No firing from Jung Lu's troops at all.

August 10. Very heavy rifle-fire from all sides about 3 A.M. A messenger sent out to meet the troops returned, bringing a letter from General Gaselee, the British general in command, also one from General Fukushima. General Gaselee's letter is dated south of Tsaitsun, August 8:

"Strong forces of allies advancing. Twice defeated enemy. Keep up your spirits."

The following letter from General Fukushima to Colonel Shiba was received:

"Camp at Changchiang, two kilometers north of Nantsaitsun, August 8, 1900—Japanese and American troops defeated the enemy on the 5th instant near Pietsang, and occupied Yangtsun on the 6th. The allied forces, consisting of American, British, Russian, and Japanese, left Yangtsun this morning, and while marching north I received your letter at 8 A.M. at a village called Nantsaitsun. It is very gratifying to learn from you that the foreign community at Peking are holding on, and believe me it is the earnest and unanimous desire of the lieutenant-general and all of us to arrive at Peking as soon as possible, and deliver you from your perilous position. Unless some unforeseen event takes place, the allied forces will be at Hoshiwu on the 9th, Mat'ou on the 10th, Changchiawan on the 11th, Tungchow on the 12th and Peking on the 13th or 14th."

The messenger who brought in the letter told the following story: On August 6 he went by way of Tungchow, finding there that his family had been murdered by the Boxers. On the 7th, he met boat-loads of wounded and defeated Chinese. At Tsaitsun he met the advance guard of the allies. The evening of the 8th he marched with the middle division to Chuanchang, six miles south of Hoshiwu. On the morning of Thursday, the 9th, he started with this division, which expected to reach Hoshiwu that evening, but left them and returned to Peking by the road to the west. The troops have but few Chinese servants. They have many pack animals, led mostly by Japs. He saw a small number of Russians and a body of several hundred mounted black (probably Bengal) lancers, who made fun and charged at him with their spears. He asked how long they would be before reaching Peking, and was told five or six days, as the Chinese were not stubbornly resisting, the allies merely having to drive them on ahead of them.

The following is an extract from a telegram received by Mr. Conger from the United States consul at Chefoo:

> "All communications north of this pass through this office. So far as known, excluding army and navy, no Americans have been killed, and there has been but little loss of property south of Tientsin. All trouble confined to Peking and Taku. The high officials are doing their best to keep order. Very large force of all nations at Taku."

August 12. Heavy firing all day.

August 13. The whole force of the artillery possessed by us was brought to bear on the Chinese position in the Mongol market, as the Chinese seem to be making a last desperate attempt to kill us all before the arrival of the relief force, and it is expected that from that quarter will come the fiercest attack.

Same date, 4 P.M. The yamen sent word that if we would refrain from firing they would positively stop all volleys on their side. This was agreed to, and five hours later, though they had been shooting all day, they made the most terrific attack of the siege. This was kept up all night, the very violent attacks being renewed at intervals of about two hours.

At 4.30 in the morning, having been up all night under the hottest fire mortals ever endured, I had just dropped asleep, which even the heavy shots did not prevent, when I was awakened by the pop, pop, pop, at regular intervals of only the fraction of a second, of an automatic gun. As I knew the Chinese had no such gun in their forces, and as our own Colt's gun was just outside the British legation gate to prevent a rush down the moat between the British legation and Lu Wang Fu, I instantly came to the conclusion that the final rush, which would end the drama and our lives, was being made.

Grasping my double-barreled shotgun, I rose from the floor, where I had just thrown myself down, and stepped outside in front of the legation chapel. As I did so I heard the thunder of heavy guns in the direction of the Tungchow gate. Then the situation was clear. The relief were outside the city engaging the Chinese troops, and the automatic gun was not ours, but theirs.

I dropped on my knees in the roadway and put up a few words of thanksgiving to Almighty God, and then, rising, called out the good news to those inside the houses, in excited tones. Oh, the sweetness of those sounds! Shall I ever forget how delightful to our ears? How anxious I felt when they ceased for a few moments, and how happy when they were resumed!

The Chinese attacking us heard them too, and for a while somewhat slackened their fire to listen; but only for a while, for they kept up a hot fire all day.

Poor Mitchell, the brave American gunner, was wounded in the night, having his arm broken by a bullet from the Mongol market attack, but he smiled a grim smile when the guns were heard outside, and remarked: "Oh, you can keep up your devilish racket now, but in a little while longer you will be silent enough!"

At about four o'clock the Americans on the wall saw men in foreign uniforms directly opposite them. While the Americans and Japanese had attacked the Tungchow stone road gate and the Pieu gate, the English had found the Shahkuo gate entirely open and unguarded, and had hastened, as directed by our notes of advice, to the water-gate, directly under the eastern extremity of the American position on the wall. The Sikhs came pouring up to the gate, which they soon smashed in, and then the hurrahs that rent the skies told those in the houses and in the hospital that the siege was over.

Just as the relief forces were pouring into the British legation, the first woman to be wounded during the siege, Mme. Cuillier, a French woman, was struck by a Mauser rifle bullet in the thigh and seriously, but not dangerously, wounded.

The following table shows the number of officers and men who were killed or wounded, and those who died of disease during the siege:

| Nationality | Number of | | Killed or died of wounds | | Wounded | | Casualties in per cent | | | Died of disease | | Volunt'rs and independents | | Total | |
|---|---|---|---|---|---|---|---|---|---|---|---|---|---|---|---|
| | Officers | Men | Officers | Men | Officers | Men | Killed | Woun'd | Total | Officers | Men | Killed | Woun'd | Killed | Woun'd |
| Am'can | 3 | 53 | .. | 7 | 2 | 8 | 12.5 | 17.8 | 30.3 | .. | .. | .. | 1 | 7 | 11 |
| Aust'an | 5 | 30 | 1 | 3 | 3 | 8 | 11.4 | 37.4 | 42.8 | .. | .. | .. | .. | 4 | 11 |
| British . | 3 | 79 | 1 | 2 | 2 | 18 | 3.7 | 24.4 | 28.1 | .. | .. | 3 | 6 | 13 | 26 |
| French . | 3 | 45 | 2 | 9 | .. | 37 | 22.9 | 77.1 | 100.0 | .. | .. | 2 | 6 | 13 | 43 |
| German | 1 | 50 | .. | 12 | .. | 15 | 23.5 | 31.4 | 54.9 | .. | .. | 1* | 1† | 13 | 16 |
| Jap'nese | 1 | 24 | .. | 5 | .. | 21 | 20.0 | 84.0 | 104.0 | .. | .. | 5‡ | 8 | 10 | 29 |
| Russian | 2 | 79 | .. | 4 | 1 | 18 | 4.9 | 23.9 | 28.3 | .. | 2§ | 1 | 1 | 7 | 20 |
| Italian.. | 1 | 28 | .. | 7 | 1 | 11 | 24.1 | 41.4 | 65.5 | .. | .. | .. | .. | 7 | 12 |
| Total | 19 | 388 | 4 | 49 | 9 | 126 | 13.1 | 35.6 | 48.7 | .. | 2 | 12 | 23 | 67 | 168 |

\* Baron Von Ketteler.  
† Mr. Cordes.  
‡ Includes Captain Anlo.  
§ Cossacks of the Legation.

# Chapter VI

WANG
Minister Conger's head servant

ONE of the most noticeable effects of siege-life has been to bring out into prominence all the mean and selfish characteristics of the individual, as well as the heroic and self-sacrificing. People who in times of peace pass for very nice, sociable individuals, with no particularly mean tendencies, when subjected to deprivation in the food-supply, and their nerves become a bit shattered with the sound of whistling bullets, the shrieking of flying shells, or the dull thud followed by the crashing and grinding of solid shot, show up in their true bedrock character, and are meanness to the core.

It has been most interesting to observe the dissolution of previous friendships, often of years' standing, and the making of new ones between individuals formerly more or less at variance. This has come about sometimes from a man or woman with a sick child, or sick member of his or her family having no supplies of their own, begging a tin of milk or a can of soup or some little delicacy or necessity from a friend having abundance of stores. Upon a flat refusal on the ground that he has none he can spare, the aforetime friend realizes the depth of the former friendship and has no wish to continue it.

Again, another instance: A gentleman has gone to inquire of a person in authority in a certain establishment, where he is to move another gentleman, a mutual friend, ill and unable to take care of himself, to a place of safety, from quarters no longer tenable, and is told: "If you have been near the sick man, keep away from me. Do what you please with him, only keep away from me and mine, as we are fearful of contagion."

"But what do you advise?" persists the inquirer of his quondam friend and superior.

"I don't advise anything," is the reply.

"Is he to be left alone to die or be captured, where he is?" still persists the anxious friend.

"That is none of my business," is the heartless answer, destroying a friendship which had existed for twenty years.

Then, too, it has been an interesting study to watch the effects on the optimistic man and the pessimistic man of the various rumors that have drifted in through occasional reports from captives or deserters from the enemy's troops.

The optimist believes that our enemies are discouraged, are short of ammunition, are fighting among themselves, are firing high purposely not to injure us; that the relief force is very near, that flashes of heat lightning are searchlights of our friends, etc.

The pessimist believes the powers are fighting among themselves to prevent relief until no one power has more troops in the relief than any other; scouts the idea of search-lights; says that the provisions are nearly exhausted; sees new barricades erected by the enemy every night; recounts the fatal casualties, increasing each day, and notes the diminishing strength of the remainder, and, moreover, fully believes and constantly asserts that we are only staving off for a little while an inevitable general massacre.

One must admit that to know that eleven of the powers of the world are kept away, or are staying away, from relieving their ministers, with their families and nationals, for two months, at a distance of only eighty miles from navigation by large vessels, is a circumstance rather calculated to increase pessimism.

Before the siege began I heard the United States minister say that if the Boxers destroyed a single station on the Peking-Hankow railroad, known popularly as the Lu Han road, they would have a horde of Cossacks protecting the line within a fortnight. Yet of the 15,000 Russians reported to have been in Port Arthur, when the entire Lu Han line and the Peking-Tientsin railroad was destroyed, not a man has as yet (August 13th) reached Peking. The Boxers are still seen from our loopholes, and make our nights hideous with their horn-blowing and incessant rifle-fire.

We were also told by those wiseacres, the foreign ministers, that Japan could and would have 50,000 men in Peking if one member of their legation was injured. Their second and third secretaries have been killed, their legation guard has been almost annihilated, and we see, as yet, no new Japanese faces.

Again, Captain Myers assured us the Americans could easily spare 10,000 men from the Philippines, who could reach Peking in, at longest, two weeks; but two months have now gone by, and they have not materialized.

The people who have, on the whole, stood the siege best are the missionaries. They have been more crowded than any others, all the Americans being compelled to occupy the British legation chapel, where they are, indeed, closely packed, while the English missionaries occupy part of the first secretary's house.

The Americans have formed into two messes, the Presbyterians and Methodists eating at one time, the Congregationalists, who are in the majority, at another. They brought in with them considerable provisions in the way of tinned stores, but have been compelled to draw from their commissariat their supply of rice and cracked wheat every day.

The foreign ministers guaranteed the three shopkeepers of Peking, Messrs. Krueger, of Kierullf & Co., Imbeck, and Chamot, the amount of their stock if they would turn it into a commissary's hands for distribution to the entire community as needed. This was at once done, and a commissary department appointed to take charge.

Many of the besieged owned ponies or mules, which were also placed under a committee, consisting of Messrs. Dering, Allardyce, and Brazier. One or two of these animals have been killed each day, and each person (foreigner) has been allowed to draw half a pound of meat. Many at first could not be persuaded to even taste horse-meat or mule-meat; but after several weeks of siege-life there were very few who did not daily go to the butchery for their supply.

The meat has been inspected every day by a physician, and a certificate of healthy flesh given to the butcher before the meat was allowed to be dispensed. One of the British marines, William Betts, of the Royal Marine Light Infantry, had been a butcher previous to enlistment, and his services have been most valuable to the entire community.

The Chinese coolies are fed with soup made from the bones, the head, and cleaned entrails. Not an ounce of the flesh has been wasted.

Many of the ponies that took part in the Peking spring meeting as racers, last May, have since served us with juicy steaks or toothsome sausages. The mule-meat is considered to be better, on the whole, than horse-meat, and in this opinion I fully concur. As we have only one donkey in the compound, none of us has as yet tried donkey-flesh; but the Chinese assure us it is even better than the larger animals.

Several days since one of the two cows in the compound, having gone dry, was killed for food, and a notice was placed on the bulletin board at the bell-tower that applications for portions of the meat would be received from all women and children, but that only such men as were wounded or ill could, upon a physician's certificate, receive a portion.

Every one wanted some, expecting to highly enjoy a taste of fresh beef and a change from horse. The result was most disappointing. The cow was old and tough, and her flesh infinitely inferior to the regular ration of horse or mule.

The Chinese Christians, supported by us in the Su Wang Fu, having been for weeks upon nothing but cracked wheat or "hao liang" gruel, were longing for some animal food, and begged they might be given some of the dogs that continued to come from all over the city to feed each night upon the refuse in the moat between the Su Wang Fu and the British legation.

A few foreigners with shotguns, therefore, sallied forth yesterday and killed eight good-sized specimens of the canine race, that were forthwith handed over to the hungry converts for their consumption. Dog-hunting as a food supply will not be neglected in the future.

As after July 18th the shelling ceased, and some of the enemies' soldiers, with an eye to business, brought a few eggs to the Japanese barricade for sale, a market department was established and placed under the care of Messrs. A. D. Brent and J. M. Allardyce, where eggs could be obtained *pro rata* for numbers of women and children in a household, compared with the supply on hand. These eggs were sold at four cents each. But often the supply only admitted of one egg being sold to a household of women or children. At other times an egg each could be obtained daily. But alas! the Chinese soldiers soon found out what their soldiers were doing, and promptly stopped it, so that after August 6th the market was obliged to close from lack of eggs.

On July 20th, two days after the shelling ceased, the tsungli-yamen sent a present to the ministers of one hundred watermelons, seventy eggplants, sixty vegetable squashes, and one hundred cucumbers. Some few of the besieged, besides the diplomats, thus obtained the first taste of fresh vegetables they had enjoyed for a month.

The ministers' request to the yamen that vegetable-venders be allowed to come to the barricades or the great gate, however, was denied, and we have since had no further supply. It is hard to know that within half a mile of us in any direction there is an abundance of fresh fruits and vegetables, and yet, owing to the closeness of our investment by the hostile troops, we cannot obtain a cent's worth.

On August 5th, while I was standing talking with a Japanese sentry, on an outpost barricade of the Su Wang Fu, a Chinese soldier in full uniform walked quickly up the narrow lane our barricade commanded toward us. I called on the Japanese to fire on him, but he remarked: "Let him come on; he has no gun, and may want to sell something."

True enough, just before reaching us he held up his hand in front of his face to indicate that he wished to speak, and so was allowed to come around the corner of the barricade. He was a young man of not over twenty-five, but showed the marks of being a confirmed opium-eater.

"I have brought you some eggs," he remarked, hastily exposing ten of the precious ovules to view. The Jap counted out forty cents and gave him, and advised him to clear out, which he speedily did, remarking as he left: "I will lose my head if I am caught at this." As he could buy the eggs in the market for five cents, his percentage of profit was very handsome.

After the so-called truce of July 18th, the native soldiers occupying the wall to the east of the American marines' barricade strictly observed the terms of the truce, and never either enlarged their barricade nor fired another shot.

These were the only ones, however, who did so. From all the other barricades we were frequently fired on, and every night or two a vigorous attack would be made upon us, during which the Chinese would expend many hundred rounds of ammunition, firing their rifles into our barricades or the roofs of our houses, and scarcely doing any damage, as we would all seek shelter until the enemy were tired out.

Only once or twice did they actually come out from behind their barricades with the intention apparently of rushing us; but upon receiving a volley, and having several killed or wounded, they would hastily bolt back again to cover.

A corner in the reception room of a wealthy
Chinese gentleman, in Peking

One night the author was selected by Adjutant Squiers to lead a company of ten coolies in an attempt to remove the stinking carcasses of two mules that had been lying festering in the rays of the summer sun for several days, directly under the noses of the American marines entrenched at foot of the city wall. The stench they emitted was overpowering, but there seemed to be no way to remove them, as to show a head, even, at the barricade was certain to bring a volley from the Chinese on the wall to the east, just beyond the moat. The situation having grown unendurable, it was necessary to risk life even to remove them, and had to be attempted.

Mr. Squiers formed the plan to have ten coolies, under a foreigner, go quietly at night through the alley-ways and court-yards that had been cut through to communicate with the American legation, to the moat directly under the Chinese on the wall. From thence we were to crawl forward toward the barricade, where our men were warned not to fire upon us, tie a rope around a mule, slip back toward the moat, and drag the mule after us, and down into the moat, where it could subsequently be covered with kerosene oil and burned.

With ten volunteer coolies, all dressed in dark clothes, and warned not to speak or even whisper, I undertook the task.

We reached the position on the wall street without incident, and I was congratulating myself we would succeed without the Chinese discovering us, when one of the coolies unfortunately struck his foot against a tin can and sent it rattling across the road. Instantly a volley was fired upon us from the Chinese barricade, only some fifty yards distant, and a perfect hail of bullets struck all about us.

"Drop on your faces and lie still," I commanded in a hoarse whisper, which was promptly obeyed.

We lay still for about fifteen minutes. Then I sent one coolie crawling on toward the nearest mule, only ten yards away, and he soon had the noose slipped over his head and returned.

We dragged the animal quietly enough, until just at the corner of the bridge, where a lot of tins, bottles, and refuse had been dumped in the early days of the siege, and before the Chinese had obtained their present position by driving the Germans from the wall in the rear of their legation.

When the animal passed over these obstacles a loud grating, rattling noise was made, and a second volley poured down from the wall. But this time the corners of the stone bridge protected us and we were in no danger.

After another wait of fifteen minutes, during which time all became quiet again, we returned and repeated the operation on the second mule, dragging his fragrant (?) carcass alongside the first, and completing our work under a third volley, equally harmless.

I received the thanks of Mr. Squiers and the entire marine guard for this service, as it rendered their position much more bearable thereafter, and their gratitude fully repaid me for the danger incurred.

Directly across a moat leading from the Imperial city wall to the southern wall of the Tartar city of Peking, opposite to the British legation, is a large square compound, known in the local mandarin tongue as Su Wang Fu, or in plain English as the palace of Prince Su.

This prince inherited the title from his father only two years ago. He is a young man of rather pleasant appearance, about thirty years of age. I have dined with him twice at the residence of his next younger brother, who was a patient of mine last winter.

This compound is surrounded by a stout brick wall from twelve to fifteen feet high. Lying, as the place does, in between the British and Austrian legations, it was decided to take possession of it for the thousand-odd Christian refugees, mostly Catholics, who had claimed the protection of their teachers, the missionaries, when the cathedrals and mission premises were burned.

The idea of doing this originated with Mr. F. H. James, who was killed on the bridge by Kansu soldiers a few days after the occupation. Dr. G. E. Morrison warmly seconded it, and the plan was carried out without opposition from Prince Su or his retainers, as actual warfare had not yet broken out.

This palace consists of a lot of rather fine (for Chinese buildings) edifices, all of one story, arranged in a series of courts, with a considerable park on the west side facing on the moat dividing the palace from the British legation.

As less than a hundred yards' space is taken up by the width of the moat and the roadway on either side, it will be readily seen that to hold this compound was to protect the entire east side of the British legation from the Chinese fire.

Colonel Shiba, the Japanese commandant, with his twenty-five soldiers, was first placed in charge, but later on he was reinforced from time to time by detachments from the Austrians, Italians, British, and French marines, and by the young men of the customs service, known as the Customs volunteers.

The most determined efforts of the siege have been made by the Chinese troops and Boxers to obtain possession of the palace—first, doubtless, because it commanded the entire east wall of the British legation at short range, and secondly, because they desired to exterminate the thousand-odd refugees—men, women, and children—harbored there. Consequently, the loss of life of our defenders and the number of wounded brought from the Su Wang Fu into the hospital has greatly exceeded that of any other one place.

To Colonel Shiba, its heroic defender, is due the greatest credit, inasmuch as he has held the place for weeks, after the other commanders had prophesied it would have to be given up in twenty-four hours.

This he has been enabled to do by building barricade after barricade in the rear of his first line of defense, at often less than fifty yards' distance, and when one barricade was shelled until absolutely untenable, retreating to the next strong position in his rear.

Colonel Shiba also enlisted all the Japanese civilians in the city, and even trained twenty-five of the native Catholic converts into very steady soldiers, arming them with rifles taken from the bodies of dead soldiers of the enemy.

In addition to the military officers who arrived with the legation guards, there happened to be in Peking at the commencement of the siege two English captains, one to study Chinese, the other representing a concession syndicate — Captains Poole and Percy Smith. Both of the gentlemen have rendered efficient and valuable service, and, since the death of Captain Strouts, have

SOUTHERN WALL OF TARTAR CITY

This picture gives an idea of the vastness of the ancient defenses of Peking and of the unhygienic character of its surroundings. Across the canal are to be seen the straggling buildings of a Tartar village. Immediately in the foreground lie the stagnant waters of the canal and piles of reeking filth.

been on regular duty.

A curious fact, interesting alike to English and Americans, is that on the Fourth of July, after Captain Myers had been wounded in the sortie on the city wall the previous night, Captain Percy Smith commanded the American marines in the trench on the wall all day, under hot fire from cannon and rifles, and the marines speak in the highest terms of his bravery and coolness, and his care for their comfort and safety.

Mr. E. von Strauch, formerly first lieutenant in the German army, but now a member of the customs service, has also rendered valuable service in relieving the officer in charge at all the various posts, such as the city wall, held by the Americans; the Su Wang Fu, held by Colonel Shiba; the Hanlin Yuan, held by the British, and other points outside the legation. The men also express the highest regard for him.

So much for the outside officers. Among civilians deserving credit are many who have daily and faithfully done the work apportioned to them in capacities where they have been unnoticed, but where their work has contributed much to the general comfort, and some of them at least should be mentioned.

Messrs. Allardyce and Brazier in the meat supply department, Mr. S. M. Russell in the commissary department, Mr. Stell in the coolie supply department, Dr. Chauncey Goodrich and Messrs. Walker and Whiting in the coolies' food supply, together with Messrs. Tewkesbury, Hobart, and Norris, all have steadily worked for the common good, often both day and night.

It has been noticed by a great many Englishmen and others that the Russians besieged with us have been of uniformly gentlemanly and courteous bearing. They have won golden opinions from all, with the exception, perhaps, of one intensely biased newspaper correspondent, who reads in the most commonplace saying some deeply-concealed meaning, and some unkind intention toward the British interests. A Russian gentleman is a perfect gentleman, and uniformly a marvelous linguist.

I have several times been present in a room with a Frenchman, a German, and an Italian, with whom several Russians carried on animated conversations, addressing each man in his own language, and apparently with equal fluency.

From M. de Giers, down through his whole legation, the professors of Russian in the Imperial University and Tung Wen Kuan, the officers and clerks of the Russo-Chinese bank, one can find none who are not perfect gentlemen and most agreeable companions.

Baron von Radew, the captain in charge of the Russian marines, has been a most devoted officer, and every point of his defenses has had his constant personal supervision. He has never undressed to sleep in the last two months, but has taken the broken rest he has obtained lying in a steamer chair in one of his barricades. He has lost greatly in flesh, and is but a skeleton of his former self, but remains the same courteous officer and gentleman under circumstances that have altered the dispositions of not a few.

If the diplomatic corps in Peking could only have heard the many and varied contemptuous remarks made about them by their own nationals, both before and during the siege, they would perhaps have a new idea of what their titles of "envoys extraordinary" meant. As I heard one gentleman remark: "After this lot are disposed of, I hope they will send us a set of 'envoys ordinary'—common-sense kind of men, who have eyes and ears."

It is certainly marvelous that with the information so readily obtainable as to the Boxer movement, its aims and intentions, and after having it forced almost upon them, as the British, American and French ministers certainly have had by their missionaries and others, the diplomatic corps should have blindly allowed themselves to be penned up in Peking with only a handful of guards, to endure treatment as disgraceful as it has been unpleasant.

True, M. Pichon urged his colleagues early to send for legation guards, and wanted them in larger numbers, but even he, after constant assurances from Bishop Faner (who was perfectly informed as to the gravity of the movement and the Imperial sanction), declined to act independently and allowed the situation to proceed to the utmost extremity before he believed the priest true and the tsung-li-yamen false.

A very blue lot they have been during the siege. Although better fed than the unfortunates—the results of their credulity—compelled to suffer with them, they have not been pleasant company, and have been allowed to flock together as birds of a feather, and discuss at length the utter neglect of their home governments in not speedily rescuing them.

The rest of us poor mortals have long since come to the conclusion that our governments have found out their true value, and have decided they are not worth a rescue.

The Belgian minister having arrived only a few weeks before the siege began, is not to blame for the position, and he wonders as much as the ordinary mortal how his colleagues could have allowed it to come to pass.

Is it possible that England and America, if they had been informed of the true state of affairs by their representatives, would not have requested their ministers to notify all the foreign women and children to leave the country?

When a foreign war is inevitable, even in a civilized country, it is a necessity for non-combatants to leave. In a barbarous country it means murder, often with torture, to remain; yet our missionaries in Paotingfu and places inland were not warned that their district troubles were not local, but general, and that they should hasten to the coast, to be nearer protection.

Some of the wiser English people among us assert that "so far from being blamed by their government for the siege, and loss of life accompanying it, their minister will be praised for bringing us safely through it, and receive a higher decoration if not a baronetcy; just as he was rewarded before for failing to keep his government informed of the Russians being the real owners of the Fu Haw railroad, receiving at that time some alphabetical additions to his signature."

John Brown is much improved by being called Sir John Brown, P.I.G. — which may mean "perfectly independent gentleman."

Posterity, however, will read of this siege with amazement, and wonder how so many blind and deaf men came to be appointed to the same post at one time. Truly a remarkable coincidence.

# Chapter VII

YOUAN CHANG
Beheaded August 9, because he favored making peace with foreigners.

THE Russian legation is situated on the north side of Legation street, directly opposite the United States legation, one hundred and fifty yards west of the moat that runs northward from the city wall to the wall of the Forbidden City; between the British legation and the Su Wang Fu. Consequently, the Russian legation is directly south of the British legation, and separated from it only by a small street containing shops of the humbler sort.

Immediately upon a state of siege being declared, the foreign guards took possession of this street, drove out the inhabitants, barricaded both ends of the highway, and so made it possible to go with safety directly from the position held by the American marines on the city wall, through the American legation, across Legation street, also barricaded, through the Russian legation, and on into the British legation — one continuous foreign occupation. This was a necessity for our protection, and to secure for the American and Russian marines a safe retreat into the British legation in the event of their own locations being no longer tenable.

At the beginning of the siege the following persons resided in the Russian legation: His Eminence M. de Giers, envoy extraordinary and minister plenipotentiary, his wife, daughter and son, and Miss Edith Miller, a governess in his family; B. N. Kroupensky, first secretary; B. N. Evreinow, second secretary; P. S. Popoff, interpreter; Mme. Popoff and five daughters; N. F. Kolessoff, second interpreter; A. T. Beltchenko and H. P. Wulff, student interpreters; V. V. Korsakoff, M.D., surgeon, wife and daughter; N. T. Gomloyeff, postmaster; A. Polyanoff, clerk in post office; the Rt.-Rev. Father Archimandrite Innocent Figuroffsky; the Rev. Father Abraham, Deacon Basile, Messrs. Osipoff and Piskimoff, ecclesiastical students. This comprised the legation personnel.

There was also the staff of the Russo-Chinese bank, consisting of the following persons: D. D. Pokotiloff, company manager for China and Japan, and his wife; D. M. Pozdneeff, his wife and child; R. T. Barbier, wife and child; Mlle. C. Titoff; E. Wihlfahrt, cashier; F. Vavier, bookkeeper; Messrs. Brackmann, Mirny, Alexandroff, Wasilieff, Brauns, and Kehler; and Mr. A. W. Borodavkine, professor of Russian in the Imperial University.

The Russian guards were sailors from the battleships Navarine and Sissoi Veliku, to the number of seventy-two men, under Naval Lieutenant Baron von Rahden and Sub-Lieutenant Carl von Dehn, with seven trans-Baikalian Cossacks.

Captain Jean Wroublevsky, who was on language-leave, also resided in the legation, and acted with Baron von Rahden alternately as commander of the forces. Captain Wroublevsky belongs to the Ninth Rifle Corps, stationed at Port Arthur.

Some of the staff of the Russo-Chinese bank served in the British legation under the orders of Captain Strouts until his death, and thereafter under Sir Claude MacDonald, who assumed command, but Messrs. Kroupensky, Evreinow, Kolessoff, Beltchenko, Dr. Korsakoff, and Professor Borodavkine constituted themselves Russian volunteers, and remained by their legation throughout the siege, never becoming a part of the so-called international volunteers serving in the British legation.

These Russian volunteers did splendid service in the defense of the Legation street west entrance, in the Mongol market to the northwest, and in the various posts and barricades on the city wall, in conjunction with the American marines.

The Russian sailors and the American marines fraternized at once; but the sailors were quite pleased to find their duties did not often bring them into contact with the British marines, for whom they felt a natural antipathy. Not that there has been the slightest disagreement or open bad blood between those two nationalities, but they seem to have been mutually pleased to remain apart.

The Russian sailors did much more manual labor than any others of the besieged. The Americans, English, French, Italians, etc., were quite satisfied to have all their barricades built for them by the Chinese Christians, working under their missionary teachers or a foreign interpreter; but the Russian sailors pitched in and built, as well as manned, all their own barricades.

Their commander, Baron von Rahden, stated that upon his arrival his men were mostly green farmers, recently enlisted as sailors, and very few of them had had any military experience or even knew the proper handling of a rifle; but after association for a few weeks with the well-trained American marines under constant fire, they had developed wonderfully fast, and he felt, at the end of the siege, that he had a body of men under him well trained, steady, and cool.

A detachment of these sailors accompanied the American marines in the expedition to the south cathedral, and assisted in the rescue of three hundred native Catholic Christians. At this place they killed seventy Boxers and took ten prisoners that they afterward handed over to the Chinese authorities for punishment; but, doubtless, instead of being punished they were well rewarded.

While these ten ruffians were confined in the legation jail, one man succeeded in getting his hands free and loosing one other. Being discovered, they assaulted their sentry with a brick and attempted to make their escape; but one being promptly shot and killed, the other surrendered and was again bound.

During the many heavy attacks by Tung Fu Hsiang's soldiers at the west end of Legation street, these sailors behaved with great courage, and with their American marine companions never failed to drive the Kansu ruffians back, until finally the Chinese became discouraged at their lack of success in rushes, and settled down to a policy of sniping from behind their heavy barricades.

They were such poor marksmen, however, that not one in a thousand of their rifle shots took effect, and the Russian losses all told amounted only to four killed and eighteen wounded.

Their outposts commanded the entire Mongol market, overlooking the southwestern wall of the British legation, and they alone commanded this district until August 5, some weeks after the active shelling had ceased, when Lieutenant Von Strauch took up a new position in the extreme north of the Mongol market, and drew some of the snipers' fire in another direction.

The Chinese, early in the siege, planted a Krupp gun on the Chien Men or main gate of the city, and from this position of vantage shelled the minister's house and other buildings of the legations very severely; but their aim was so bad that many of their shells passed not only over the Russian legation, but over the British legation and Su Wang Fu as well, finally falling or exploding among their own people more than a mile away from their intended target.

Doubtless more Chinese have been killed by their own shells and rifles than we have killed. As they always fired high, and completely surrounded us, the balls that have constantly whistled over our heads for two months must have fallen among themselves.

They attribute to our good shooting a large mortality that we know is a result, certainly in part, of their bad shooting. In the sortie made on the city wall the night of July 3d under Captain Myers, which resulted in capturing the Chinese barricades, several banners, and some ammunition, the Russian sailors ably seconded the United States marines.

Captain Wroublevsky on one side found it impossible to pass in, and joined the marines in forcing entrance into the other side. In this sortie Baron von Rahden was struck on the head with a brick and two sailors were wounded. Of the Americans, Captain Myers was severely wounded and two marines killed.

Some of the best work of the Russians was that done in burning many native houses and then pulling down the walls in the Mongol market that concealed sharpshooters of the enemy. Had this not been done, the entire southwestern part of the British legation would have been under a constant sniping fire, such as they really were exposed to during the first few days of the siege, and until the Russians made a dash into the Mongol market, drove out the Chinese, and burned down their cover.

The Russians also joined in an unsuccessful sortie, during which an attempt was made to capture a cannon in the Su Wang Fu, but owing to incorrect information as to its whereabouts, the

ON TOP OF CHINA'S GREAT WALL

Wall destroyed by the Russians after the Boxers got it. This picture gives a good idea of the width of the Great Wall, and looks almost like a field with vegetation growing, and the block-house or fort erected upon it. The method of reaching the top of the wall is shown by the driveway up the side, which it will be observed, is completely commanded by the block-house. This wall extends several thousand miles, and is said to represent the sacrifice of millions of lives, and labor beyond comprehension.

Italian officer commanding led his men in the wrong direction, and after having several men wounded, the party returned without having accomplished anything.

In the fortification of their own legation they have been untiring, and besides loop-holing and building barricades, have dug a very deep trench all along inside their west wall, or only exposed side, which effectually prevented underground mines from being undetected.

Russian sentries have, all through the siege, been posted on the moat bridge at Legation street, commanding the water-gate under the city wall. Curiously enough, no attack has ever been made from this quarter, yet to a foreigner it appears a most advantageous opening for attack.

The Russo-Chinese bank was held by the volunteers as long as it was possible to hold it, but after the Chinese built a high barricade on the wall just over the bank, it grew too hot to hold and had to be evacuated.

Mr. Wihlfahrt's house, directly under the wall, was made a Chinese fort for a while, and the Americans lost several men from snipers posted there, until, finally, a rush was made and the place destroyed.

The Russians have several times gone to other places to assist in repelling serious attacks, on one occasion to help Colonel Shiba in holding back the Boxer forces at the Su Wang Fu. On this occasion one man was seriously wounded. Another time they were called to help the German legation. They have always cheerfully rendered any assistance when called upon, and Baron von Rahden, his fellow officers, and all the volunteers are highly thought of by the besieged.

Few people are aware that when all the troops had left their outposts and retired into the British legation, owing to a mistaken order, four Russian sailors still remained alone at a barricade commanding the Mongol market, and by keeping the Chinese soldiers from being aware of the general retreat into the legation, made it possible for the guards to return to the American, French, and German legations and the wall, which otherwise could only have been done at a frightful cost of lives.

The United States legation, usually spoken of as the American legation, is pleasantly situated on the south side of Legation street. It is, however, a very small compound. There is only one building in it of foreign style of architecture, utilized as a business office. The second secretary had his residence in the upper portion of this building.

At the commencement of the siege the following persons were residing in the compound: His Eminence E. H. Conger, minister, his wife, daughter, niece, governess, and two lady guests from Chicago, Mrs. and Miss Woodward; Mr. H. G. Squiers, first secretary, his wife and four sons; Mr. W. E. Bainbridge, second secretary, and his wife; Mr. F. D. Cheshire, interpreter. These comprised the legation staff.

There were also the following refugees, who had been obliged to abandon their residences and seek legation asylum: Dr. W. A. P. Martin, president of the Imperial University and author of the "Cycle of Cathay," "Hanlin Papers," and other works, both in English and Chinese; Dr. Robert Coltman, Jr., professor of surgery in the Imperial University, author of "The Chinese — Medical, Political and Social," with his wife and six children; Mr. William N. Pethick, secretary to Li Hung Chang, and three American missionary ladies, Mrs. Mateer, Miss Douw, and Miss Brown.

In Mr. Squiers' family there was also a visitor of distinction — Miss Condit-Smith, a niece of Chief Justice Field, of the United States Supreme Court — as well as a French and a German nursery governess.

The marine guard of fifty men was under the command of Captains Myers and Hall, who, with Surgeon Lippett, constituted the officers of the detachment. Captain Hall, with twenty marines, had been for several days at the Methodist mission compound, east of the Hatamen or extreme southeast gate of the city, but on June 20, when it was decided to abandon that compound, and have the American missionaries all move into the British legation, Hall and his men returned to the American legation and thereafter served there. The fatigue endured by the United States marines in their constant service on the city wall and in their barricade under the wall, as well as the barricade at the western end of the compound in Legation street, was simply killing. That the men did not succumb is a marvel.

To Mrs. H. G. Squiers, more than any one else, is due the credit of sustaining them with coffee and biscuits sent out hot and refreshing at midnight and at various times throughout the day. Indeed this lady has acquired, by her hospitality and unfailing kindness, the affection of not only her own nationals, but the regard of every one besieged within the city. Many poor fellows wounded in the hospital have blessed her with their fevered lips for a cooling drink or a nourishing broth prepared by her own hands. Her well-furnished storeroom was placed at the disposal of every one who was in need of food, either as a necessity for the healthy or a delicacy for the sick. The author has to express his own unbounded gratitude for many a tin of peas, tomatoes, or oatmeal that has helped to render palatable the daily ration of horse-flesh and rice that has been his own and his family's sustenance throughout our imprisonment.

Under the most trying circumstances Mrs. Squiers has preserved a cheerful demeanor, and, assisted by the ever calm and always sociable Miss Polly Condit-Smith, has daily entertained at her hospitable board the officers, civilians, diplomats, and missionaries with the same cordiality.

When Dr. Velde, the able German surgeon in charge of the hospital, was worn out with fatigue and unable to find a quiet place for a night's rest, he was provided by Mrs. Squiers with a comfortable pallet, covered with a mosquito curtain, in a little closet room, usually occupied by the German nurse, and so enabled to obtain a rest that was an absolute necessity to his continuing in service.

All of the American ladies have worked with patience and

perseverance, constantly making the sand-bags which have so efficiently protected the soldiers and the entire community from the unceasing fire of bullets from the enemy. Everything in the line of cloth has been used for this purpose. Handsome linen table-cloths, rich silk draperies, towels, gowns and dress materials have been freely sacrificed to provide for the defense.

When the wounded became numerous in our quarters, and were nightly worried by those infernal pests, the mosquitoes, the ladies cheerfully sent all their mosquito curtains to the hospital to be used by their brave defenders to alleviate their discomfort.

Every one realized when we became besieged that we were in a position that only divine help and a speedy rescue could avail us. Surrender under any circumstances now could only mean butchery. We had seen the survivors of the massacre at the south cathedral come among us with little children almost hacked to pieces by the cruel knives of the fanatical Boxers, and, knowing their hatred for us, we well knew that if the men were overcome, the women and children must suffer a horrible death or worse.

Many of the men had resolved that at the last fight they would themselves kill their wives and daughters to prevent their suffer-

A corner in the United States Legation

ing at the hands of the incarnate devils that surrounded us. My own wife never allowed me to leave her upon a night-attack without first giving her my revolver for the purpose of using it as a safeguard to herself and daughters in the event of my non-return, and the overpowering of our forces.

The American marines led in the expedition to the south cathedral to rescue the Catholic Christians being killed there, and were accompanied by a Russian detachment and by civilians W. N. Pethick and W. J. Duysberg. Here they rescued over three hundred Christians, and brought them safely to the American legation, where their wounds were dressed by Drs. Lippett, Korsakoff, and Coltman, and they were then sent into the Su Wang Fu to be fed and cared for until the end of the siege.

The American marines also took part in the expedition to the Boxer rendezvous temple, north of the Austrian legation, in which fifty-six Boxers were cornered and killed. Their bravery and endurance has been noted by all. Their main task—that of holding the city wall—should render their fame immortal. True, they have been ably helped in this task from time to time by both Russian and British marines, but the post was theirs, and to them belongs preëminently the glory of holding the position that, like the Su Wang Fu, was a key to the place of last stand—the British legation.

In the brilliant sortie on the night of July 3, led by Captain Myers, both Russian and British marines took part, and, although the credit has usually been attributed to the Americans, English and Russians are equally deserving. When on the point of springing over our barricade to attack the Chinese position, Captain Myers addressed his men with ringing words of encouragement.

The Chinese had their first intimation of his movement when they were saluted with a deafening yell directly under their barricade, for our little force gave a tremendous shout, as instructed, as they rushed around the one open side and clambered over the breastwork.

Many of the Chinese fled, but the remainder poured a hot fire into the ranks of the invaders, Privates Turner and Thomas of the Americans being instantly killed by bullets, as reported, and Captain Myers severely wounded by a spear. Corporal Gregory of the British marines was also shot, and two Russian soldiers were wounded by bullets; but the position was captured, and the retention of the post on the wall assured, as henceforth it would be possible to ascend the ramp without being exposed to Chinese fire.

The Chinese fled to their second barricade, a few hundred yards nearer the Chien Men, which they have held ever since, and, although they have shelled the American position captured from them for days, they have never been able to dislodge our men.

When the United States minister and his family left the legation and sought refuge in the British legation, they were given the house of the British legation physician, Dr. Poole, for a residence, and into this six-roomed house were crowded four men, ten women and nine children.

Mr. Squiers, Mr. Cheshire, and Mr. Pethick continued to remain at the United States legation. The legation building was peppered with bullets the livelong day, and shelled at intervals with three-inch shells from both city gates, east and west, until all the roofs were full of holes, and the gatehouse completely demolished, the flagstaff being cut through and the flag falling to the ground. It was speedily picked up, however, and nailed to a tall tree near the gatehouse, from which it still floats, though riddled with holes.

Dr. Lippett, the surgeon of the guard, received a bad wound of the thigh, fracturing the bone and completely disabling him, on June 29, and has been in the hospital ever since. Dr. G. D. Lowry, a medical missionary of the Methodist mission, immediately took his place.

Sergeant Fanning, Corporal King, and Privates Kennedy, Tutcher, and Fisher have been killed in the barricades, and Privates Silva, Shroder, Mueller, and Hall were wounded early in the siege. The Americans killed were all buried in the Russian legation compound just across Legation street.

There were no American civilians serving as volunteers with the American guard, but Dr. Coltman, his son, Robert Coltman, 3rd, and Mr. W. E. Bainbridge served guard-duty in the British legation among the international volunteers.

Mr. H. G. Squiers, who was elected by Sir Claude MacDonald

as his chief of staff, and second in command after the death of Captain Strouts, has been indefatigable in his service, not only at the American legation, but in general oversight of the situation at all points. That the United States government will recognize his unusual ability by a promotion in the diplomatic service, for which he is so well fitted, and to which he has devoted his talents, is sincerely hoped.

He it was who conceived the plan of occupying the city wall and insisted on its being regained when abandoned. This, as a key to the whole position, was recognized in its full importance by Mr. Squiers. He, too, with Captain Wroublevsky, forced a way down the wall to the Chien Men, and let in the first Sikhs that came through the gate.

# Chapter VIII

TYPICAL CHINESE LION
As represented by them. One of a pair
guarding a temple entrance.

AT the same time that the tsung-li-yamen sent dispatches to each of the foreign ministers requesting them to leave Peking within twenty-four hours, they sent a communication to Sir Robert Hart, Bart., inspector-general of customs, notifying him of their communication to the ministers. One would have supposed that the customs staff, being employed by the government to collect their own revenues, would have either been given a place of safety and separated from the foreigners who were to be attacked and exterminated, or their safe escort out of the country guaranteed.

This should also have applied to the staff of the Imperial University, but beyond a simple notification to Sir Robert Hart, no further account was taken of them, and they were left to seek either the protection of their respective legations, or remain together in the offices of the inspector-general, where all had gathered upon the entrance of the Boxers into Peking, and attempt to defend their lives and those of their families as best they might.

As the Austrians had been driven out of their legation before any of the others had yielded, and as their compound overlooked and commanded the inspectorate-general compound, however, that place had become untenable by June 20, and Sir Robert Hart reluctantly retired with all his staff and their families to a building allotted to them in the British legation.

This building is situated just within the main gate of the legation, north of and adjoining the gate-house, and consists of three fair-sized and three small rooms, with an out-house kitchen.

Into this narrow accommodation the following staff were obliged to crowd themselves: Sir Robert Hart, inspector-general; Mr. Robert E. Bredon, deputy inspector-general, his wife and daughter, Miss Juliet Bredon; Mr. A. T. Piry, commissioner, his wife, governess, and four children; Mr. J. R. Brazier, his wife and two children; Mr. C. H. Brewit-Taylor and wife; Mr. C. H. Oliver, sister, and two children; Mr. S. M. Russell and wife, and Mr. C. B. Mears and wife, besides the following single gentlemen: Messrs. P. von Rautenfeld, J. H. Macoun, J. W. Richardson, E. Wagner, E. von Strauch, N. Konoraloff, B. L. Simpson, H. P. Destelan, H. Bismarck, U. F. Wintour, J. H. Smyth, J. W. H. Ferguson, L. Sandercock, A. G. Bethell, L. de Luca, C. L. Lauru, R. B. de Courcy, C. O. M. Diehr, W. S. Dupree, E. E. Encamacao, J. de Pinna, P. J. Oreglia, and S. Sugi.

As it was simply impossible for all these people to sleep within such narrow quarters, Messrs. Brazier and Brewit-Taylor and their families secured rooms with some friends at other houses. The remainder all messed together, excepting Mr. Bredon's family, in which were included Messrs. B. L. Simpson and C. L. Lauru. The single men slept in blankets on the narrow brick veranda when not on duty at one of the many posts.

With the exception of Sir Robert Hart, whose advanced age prevented his doing military duty, and Mr. R. E. Bredon and Mr. C. H. Oliver, all the others regularly enrolled themselves as a volunteer corps known as the customs volunteers, and did most excellent, arduous, and effective work.

Mr. E. von Strauch, having served as first lieutenant in the

German army for some years, was given command, and Mr. Macoun was made second officer. After Macoun was wounded, and until again able to go on duty, Mr. B. L. Simpson acted as second officer.

Adjoining the British legation on the north lies the Hanlin Yuan, a large yard full of many buildings, containing one of the most famous libraries extant, the Hanlin library. By the Chinese this library has always been regarded as one of their most valuable possessions. Here were stored thousands of volumes of Chinese history, essays, and records of the various government boards that had collected for centuries. North of this Hanlin Yuan, separated only by a wide street known as the Chang An Chieh, is the wall of the Forbidden City.

The Boxers and Imperial troops early took possession of the northern end of this compound, and in their efforts to dislodge us from the British legation, ruthlessly set fire to their sacred library and destroyed the priceless collections of ages.

A large part of the defense of the southern half of the Hanlin Yuan has been performed by the customs volunteers, and there has been no more trying military service in the siege than at that place. We early took possession of the southern end, and built a barricade of bricks and sand-bags running completely across the compound.

Our barricade and the Chinese barricades are so close that often the Chinese have thrown half bricks over at us, as their rifle-bullets cannot penetrate the barricade. Several of our men have been injured by stones and bricks in this way.

In addition to the members of the customs staff given above as enrolled members of the customs volunteers, there have been attached to the corps for duty at various times Messrs. Barbier, Flicke, and Hagermann.

Messrs. E. Wagner and H. P. Destelan were soon called to serve at the French legation, as the fighting had been very hot there, and men were needed to take the places of those who had fallen. They barely joined their fellow-nationals at their perilous post, and there on July 1 Wagner was struck by a shell in the head and instantly killed. A few days later Destelan had a miraculous escape. The Chinese across the narrow lane, known as Customs lane, had undermined the street, and placed a mine under the wall and eastern buildings of the legation. When they exploded it, Destelan and several others were buried in the ruins; but a second explosion almost immediately blew several of them out again, among them Destelan and Von Rosthorn, the Austrian *chargé d'affaires*, who was on duty in the French legation after the surrender of his own legation to the Chinese troops. Only two Frenchmen lost their lives by this mine, while the Chinese acknowledge they lost twenty of their own men by the explosion.

The sad death of Wagner threw a deep gloom for many days over his young comrades in arms. He was so intelligent, bright and cheerful, always willing to undertake any service, and always in the front, that he has been sorely missed. Mr. H. Bismarck was obliged by the necessities of the German legation to join his nationals there, as was also Mr. Diehr.

Bismarck has had his hat shot off and his clothes perforated several times, has been in several sorties and all sorts of dangers, but has wonderfully escaped.

Mr. L. de Luca received a painful, but not serious, wound of the forearm, which partially disabled him for a time; but, as soon as possible, he was again serving at the various posts. For a time he was on Captain Wray's staff as aid in the commissary department, but in this place there was no danger to be incurred, and he joyfully relinquished it to Mr. C. H. Oliver.

Mr. J. W. Richardson was the first of the customs volunteers to be disabled, having received, early in the siege, a flesh-wound of the shoulder. He, too, made a rapid recovery, and was soon acting as assistant steward in the hospital, but when entirely in health returned again to guard duty.

Mr. A. G. Bethell became ill from overwork and fatigue, and was obliged to go into the hospital for several days, but recovered under rest and appropriate treatment and returned to duty.

Mr. U. F. Wintour, while excavating a deep trench in the Hanlin Yuan as a countermine to the Chinese mining attempts, badly sprained his knee-joint, which has since resulted in a severe synovitis, compelling him to remain with his leg fixed in a plaster-of-paris cast for some weeks.

Messrs. Sandercock, Bethell, and Ferguson, although barely nineteen years of age, have endured the fatigue and hardship of the watches, and have been as cool under fire as old veterans.

Especial mention should be made of the conspicuous bravery and gallantry of Mr. W. S. Dupree, or, as he is familiarly and affectionately called by his comrades, "Little Willie." This young man, in times of peace, is a postal clerk of very affable manners, but in the siege he has been a doughty warrior. Although only eighteen years of age, he has taken his full share of the work. He accompanied the first expedition of the American, British, and Austrian soldiers in the attack upon a Boxer rendezvous in a temple north of the Austrian legation, in which fifty-six Boxers were killed. He has also served in the Hanlin Yuan, in the Su Wang Fu, and in the latest achievement of the customs volunteers, — the capture and holding of a new and valuable strategical position northward of the Russian position in the Mongol market.

On the night of August 10 this intrepid youngster crept out

Chinese barber at work

from behind the fortification in the Mongol market, and crawled across the moonlit common, directly in front of and up to the Chinese barricade. Here he heard one of the soldiers exhorting his comrades to follow him and make an attack upon the foreigners. "Why should we hesitate?" he urged. "We have so many and they so few success is sure and failure impossible." Dupree hurried back and warned his companions in time to prevent a serious rush, for a few moments later the Chinese actually left their barricade and attempted a rush upon our works; but on a volley into them, which killed one and wounded several others, their short-lived courage left them, and they precipitately bolted back again behind shelter, from which they peppered our barricade vigorously for the next half hour without doing any damage.

The customs mess, in spite of their exceedingly narrow accommodations, was eminently a hospitable group, and cheerfully allowed Messrs. E. Backhouse, G. P. Peachey, Dr. J. Dudgeon, and J. M. Allardyce to eat with them, they turning the stores they possessed on entrance into the common storeroom. The meals were well managed under the efficient care of Mrs. Russell and Mrs. Mears, whom all of the customs volunteers will ever remember for their constant, untiring efforts to render palatable the daily ration of horse-meat and rice which has constituted their principal food.

Sir Robert Hart, the I. G., as he is generally spoken of by his staff, as well as many outsiders, has endeared himself to all his young soldiers by his sharing with them without complaint and unvarying cheerfulness the meager diet of the mess. He has never allowed any delicacy supplied to him that the others did not partake of, but has acted on the principle of share and share alike throughout. He may in time have a successor in the service, but he can never be supplanted in the affections of those members of his staff who have endured with him the trials of the siege in Peking.

Mr. J. H. Smyth entered the British legation when he was convalescing from scarlet fever, and was placed in quarantine for some weeks. Consequently he was prevented from taking any part in the early proceedings of the siege, but as soon as allowed out he at once went on duty. Mr. Origlia came down with scarlet fever also on July 10, and thereafter could render no military service.

The staff of the British legation who were actually in the siege consisted of the following persons: Sir Claude M. MacDonald, G. C. M. G., K. C. B., envoy extraordinary, etc., his wife, two children, and sister-in-law; Herbert G. Dering, secretary; Henry Cockburn, Chinese secretary, and wife; W. P. Ker, assistant Chinese secretary, wife, and child; Wordsworth Poole, M.D., surgeon; B. G. Tours, accountant, wife, and child; D. Oliphant, consular assistant; W. Russell, consular assistant; Rev. W. Norris, acting chaplain; Rev. R. Allen, curate, and the following student interpreters. Messrs. T. G. Hancock, A. T. Flaherty, H. Bristow, T. C. C. Kirke, H. Porter, W. M Hewlett, A. Rose, R. Drury, L. R. Barr, H. Warren, L. Giles, W. E. Townsend. Captain F. G. Poole, who was living with his brother, the doctor, while on language-leave, was also considered of the legation household, as well as several guests, Mr. Clarke-Thornhill and the legation keeper, Sergeant R. Herring.

The military guard consisted of Senior Captain B. M. Strouts, Captains Halliday and E. Wray, Sergeants J. Murphy, A. E. Saunders and J. Preston; four corporals, one bugler, one armorer, and one hospital steward, with sixty-eight privates. They had one Nordenfeldt quick-firing gun. The greater part of the civilians serving as volunteers also served under Captain Poole in the British legation.

When the siege commenced, the western side at the south end of the compound, which adjoined a lot of Chinese buildings, was a most vulnerable point, which the natives readily discovered, and a number of vigorous attempts to set fire to the legation were made by firing these buildings, so that a fire-brigade was organized under B. G. Tours and Tweed, of the volunteers, to fight this dangerous form of attack.

During one of these fires in the first few days of the siege,

Captain Halliday led a brilliant rush through a hole knocked in the wall, and drove off the attacking party, killing over twenty of them. Unfortunately Captain Halliday was severely wounded by a shot through the lungs, which rendered him helpless, and lost to the besieged the services of a brave and kindly officer.

The British marines took part in the expedition to the Boxer rendezvous and the taking of the city wall, where Sergeant Murphy distinguished himself as the leader after the fall of Captain Myers. Brave Captain Strouts, who was much loved by his men, was shot and mortally wounded in the Su Wang Fu on July 16, while on a tour of inspection. Dr. G. E. Morrison was injured by the same volley, and Colonel Shiba, who was with them, narrowly escaped, several bullets passing through his clothing.

The British legation compound being of such dimensions, necessitated a larger guard for lookouts than any other one place. Notwithstanding this, men were daily detached for duty with the Americans on the city wall, and to help Colonel Shiba in the Su Wang Fu. A barricade was built across the moat connecting the legation with the Fu, and thus the men could cross without being seen from the north bridge just under the Forbidden City walls, where a strong force of the enemy was posted. To replace these detachments sent out, the civilian volunteers were largely called upon, and rendered excellent service.

Sir Claude MacDonald, after the death of Captain Strouts, assumed command of the garrison, and directed some of the outposts of other nationals; but the French and Germans denied his authority at their outposts, and controlled their own movements. Captain Poole was in charge of the international volunteers within the British legation and had command of the north stables, north wall, Hanlin Yuan, and students' quarters. He led one expedition into the carriage-park, a large tract of land which came close to the legation on the northwest side of our enclosure.

As will be seen from the accompanying diagram of the British legation, the eastern side and the southern side required no watches kept so long as the Japanese retained possession of the

Su Wang Fu and the Russians and Americans held the wall and Legation street. But the Hanlin Yuan in the north and the entire western wall covered long stretches of space that required a constant watch to be kept, as the Chinese were intrenched in numerous and heavy barricades in their front, from which they maintained a constant fire from rifles, Krupp guns and smooth-bore cannon.

Until the 18th of July the cannons boomed from morning until night, sending their solid shot and shrieking shells into our midst, tearing the brick houses to pieces, and crushing the tiles on the roof to fine powder, at the same time sending their fragments in every direction. The very shortness of range prevented their dropping with any force, and saved us much damage; and when the muzzles of their pieces were raised to pass over the first row of buildings, which they had failed to batter down, the projectiles flew harmlessly over our heads.

The building that has suffered most has been the constable's house, in the south stables. This place has borne the brunt of most of the attacks made upon the British legation and is literally converted into a sieve.

Under the direction of Mr. F. D. Gamewell all the walls of the legation have been so strengthened, often to a thickness of eight feet, that one is perfectly safe behind them, except at the loopholes, and in these large bricks are kept, except when the openings are being used for observation or firing.

The Chinese have been remarkably bad marksmen, and have usually fired by holding their guns up so that the point barely projected above their barricades, and then, pressing the trigger, immediately withdrawing the gun, having never ventured their lives in the least. But this method of firing does no damage. Thousands upon thousands of bullets have been sent whistling far over our heads. Doubtless when we hear the history of the outside we will learn of hundreds having been killed and wounded a long way from the legation district.

On July 5 Mr. David Oliphant, of the legation staff, while serving in the Hanlin Yuan, was shot in the abdomen and died from shock and internal hemorrhage in about an hour. Brief mention of his death has previously been made. He was born on July 12, 1876, and had been three years in the consular service. Passing first in his examination, he soon showed a special aptitude for acquiring the Chinese language, so much so that when he finished his term of student interpreter he was retained to work as consular assistant in the chancery of the British legation.

Here his services have been appreciated most highly by those under whom he worked, and his loss is a most grievous blow to all those who came officially in contact with him.

He was one of the most promising of the younger members of the British consular service, with which he was further connected in the person of his uncle, Mr. R. M. Mansfield, H. B. M. consul at Amoy. During his stay in Peking, David Oliphant had endeared himself to all who knew his exceptionally even temper, readiness to oblige, and active mind. In sport he was the leading spirit and manager, and he will be practically impossible to replace in this capacity.

When the siege began he was among the first to go forward in the defense of the legations. Untiringly he worked at fortifications, vigilantly he watched at night. When a portion of the Hanlin Yuan was occupied he was specially detailed for service there, and took part in several brilliant raids in connection with the occupation.

It was while cutting down a tree here in an advanced position that he was struck down by the enemy's bullet, and his promising career cut short. He died in the arms of his elder brother, Nigel Oliphant, of the Imperial Bank of China. He is deeply and sincerely mourned by all who knew him.

Another young man, Mr. H. Warren, student-interpreter, while on duty in the Su Wang Fu, on July 16, was struck by a shell in the face; he was very badly injured and died in a few hours.

# Chapter IX

August F. Chamot

THE Austro-Hungarian detachment consisted of thirty bluejackets from the cruiser Zenta. They arrived in Peking on June 3 by the last train, together with the German detachment. Lieutenant T. Kollar was in command, with Midshipman Baron R. Boyneburg von Lengsfeld and T. Mayer. With the detachment arrived also Captain Thomann von Montalmar and Lieutenant Ritter von Winterhalter, so that there were five officers and thirty men at Peking. When communication was cut Captain Montalmar took command himself.

In the legation there were only Dr. A. von Rosthorn and Mrs. von Rosthorn, the minister having left on leave in April and Vice-consul Natiesta being sick at Shanghai. His successor, Mr. Gottwald, tried to come up in the relief expedition under Admiral Seymour. The detachment guarded also the Belgian legation until the Belgian minister left there, and came to the Austrian legation on June 16.

On June 13, a Boxer attack on the new mint and the Imperial Bank of China was checked by rifle-fire from the east corner of the legation. A second attack was made at night and was also repulsed. During the search following the unsuccessful attack, several Boxers were killed a few hundred yards to the north on

Customs street.

The next day the traffic on the Chang An street crossing Customs street was stopped by an outpost, and later on by a wire fence, in order to prevent the smuggling of disguised Boxers into the legation quarter.

During the night the guard at the Belgian legation was attacked, but beat off the Chinese. A patrol caught some suspicious people, who were handed over to the Chinese authorities. A part of the French detachment assisted them in their night watches at the barracks.

On June 20, the detachment was ready for marching, to escort Dr. and Mrs. von Rosthorn, as no notice had been given to Dr. von Rosthorn of the ministers' new decision not to leave. On arriving, about 3 P.M., at the French legation, Dr. von Rosthorn was shown by Mr. Pichon a letter from the tsung-li-yamen to the ministers, promising them protection. Upon this, Dr. von Rosthorn returned with the detachment to the Austrian legation.

While all the posts were being reoccupied, and the bluejackets began to re-erect the fortifications, which had been pulled down before leaving to prevent the Chinese from using them, Tung Fu Hsiang's soldiers, who were well hidden in the neighboring houses, opened a fierce firing from two sides at about 3.30 P.M.

The Austrian legation being entirely exposed, and untenable against any serious attack, it had been understood that the *chargé d'affaires* and the detachment were to retreat to the French legation. This was done under a galling fire, but there was only one man wounded.

The Austrians immediately hastened to a position in the barrier erected by the French some one hundred yards south of the customs compound. From that day they defended with the French the French legation.

The Austrian legation, after having been looted, was burned by the Chinese on June 21. On June 22, the fire extended to the houses on both sides of the barricade, and the latter had to be left. Another one was built near the corner of Customs and Legation streets commanding Customs street.

On June 22, owing to a false alarm, the Italian, French, and German legations were left, but were almost immediately rein-habited, with the exception of the Italian legation, which was al-ready burning, as was also their wall of defense commanding the east end of Legation street.

From that date Captain von Montalman directed the fighting of both the French and the German legations, Sir Claude Mac-Donald having at that time been elected by the ministers as their commander-in-chief.

The attacks on the French legation were, from the beginning, extremely vehement, as the Chinese fully recognized the high importance of its position. Had it been lost, the German lega-tion, the Hotel de Peking, and the Su Wang Fu would have been no longer tenable. The Austrians shared in all the various ser-vices which the garrison of the French legation had to perform. A strong barricade was built to command East Legation street, and a sort of blockhouse was erected at the main gate.

Together with the French and Germans several successful dashes were made in the neighborhood, killing and wounding a number of Chinese each time.

On June 24 a detachment under Midshipman William Boy-neburg took part with the Germans in storming the city wall, which enabled the Americans to reoccupy their former position on the top. The Austrians constantly reinforced the Germans on the wall-front to the east, and after the 26th of June constantly had five men assisting Colonel Shiba at the Su Wang Fu. Their machine-gun did excellent service as long as the position behind the barricades could be maintained, and after this was given up it was sent from time to time to Russian, German, and English legations as needed.

When the French legation was under the hottest fires from north, east, and south, only the western side being protected by the other legations, the French took the northern and the Austri-ans the southern line of defense, and were each under constant rifle-shot at only twenty-five yards' range. This they endured for weeks. On June 29 the Chinese succeeded in making a break in the eastern wall on Customs street, and set fire to the French legation stables; but they had not sufficient courage to follow up the advantage gained with a rush. But this necessitated relinquishing the barrier in the southern end of Customs street and easternmost line of cover in Legation street, the garrisons being under rear and flank fire.

The Chinese were gaining daily, or rather nightly, in making the breaches in the eastern wall larger and more numerous, until they had nearly razed the entire structure. Yet they gained no great advantage, owing to the breaches being so well covered from the windows of buildings and temporary defenses in the western part of the compound.

The fatigue endured by our people was most extraordinary. From July 1 daily shelling was endured, which riddled the roofs and walls of every building in the compound, until the principal building and main gateway, an imposing structure, were utterly demolished and became a pile of ruins.

On the 8th of July the Chinese brought into position at about eighty yards' distance a three-inch Krupp gun, from which they commenced to pour in a destructive fire on the eastern wall. Captain Von Thornburg, with Captain Labrousse and Lieutenants Darcy and Kollar, all anxious to locate this gun exactly, left their main barricade and proceeded to a spot behind a low loopholed wall in their front, but had scarcely arrived when a shell burst in their midst, a fragment of which pierced Von Thornburg through the heart, causing him to fall dead into the arms of his friends. He was sorrowfully carried to the rear, and at 2 P.M. was buried with military honors, although the bullets were falling thick around those who were thus honoring their comrade and leader. The tears of sympathy on this occasion evidenced the sorrow of the men, and the general esteem in which the fallen had been held.

After the death of Captain Von Thornburg, the command of

the Austrians devolved upon Lieutenant Von Winterhalter.

On July 13, at 6:45 P.M., the Chinese made a furious attack, commencing with rifle-fire and shouts of "Kill! Kill!" This was intended to draw all the defenders into their positions, and nearly succeeded, for after a few moments the rifle-fire suddenly ceased and two mines exploded with a great report, blowing up Mr. Morisse's house, where Dr. Von Rosthorn, Lieutenant Darcy, and Mr. Destelan, with four French sailors, were stationed. Two of the sailors were never recovered, but all the others were able to extricate themselves from the ruins with but slight injuries.

Earth, stones, and dust were thrown high into the air, clouds of heavy, sulphurous smoke rose from the hole in the ground, poisoning the dust-laden air, and, at the same moment, to add to the horror of the situation, two three-inch guns opened up on the main gate house, sending in their contingent of iron hail from a distance of only eighty yards.

This explosion compelled both the Austrians and French to retire about thirty yards eastward behind a cover they had already partly erected in preparation for a stubbornly contested retreat; but upon the shell-fire ceasing, the combined forces made a rush later on, drove the Chinese out of the main gateway, and reoccupied it.

Never in history has there been a more stubbornly contested few acres than those occupied by the Austrians and French in the French legation compound. The buildings, however, taking fire, the French were compelled to retire again behind their intrenchment in the western part of the garden, the Austrians retreating to the chapel and earthworks connecting with the *Pavilion des Etrangers*, a small building with very thin walls. One small house was burned by the Austrians to prevent the Chinese from using it against them.

At first this entire new line of defense was very weak, but it was rapidly strengthened by adding bricks and sand-bags. Yet even to the end all visitors considered it a very precarious defense. One American marine remarked, "Our place is bad enough, but this is worse."

As the Chinese barricaded themselves in the western part of the legation captured by them, they also made use of the shrubbery and trees to shield their force, and these the Austrians had to clear away under hot fire. Until July 17, day and night, the enemy in the opposite barriers poured in a steady fire, which the Austrians only returned by an occasional shot, as their ammunition had to be husbanded.

The so-called truce did not last very long, for on the 23d the firing was nearly as bad as before, and at night often worse. To cut off any further mines, a trench sixty yards long and ten feet deep was dug in front of the *Pavilion des Etrangers*. As was afterward seen, the Chinese had really attempted two further mines, but for some unknown reason had given up before they were completed.

On the last night of the siege the firing in the French legation, as everywhere else, was exceedingly hot, and, although two shells burst in the chapel, no one was injured.

The Austrians lost: killed, one officer, three bluejackets; wounded, three officers, eight bluejackets. Of the 10,000 rounds of ammunition brought to Peking 2,000 were used by the men, and 2,000 by the machine-gun. The shield of the machine-gun shows the marks of having been struck by rifle-balls some fifty-odd times.

No story of the siege in Peking would be complete without mention of the work of August Chamot and his heroic wife. He is a Swiss, and in Peking has charge of the Hotel de Peking for Messrs. Tallieu & Co. His wife is a San Francisco girl.

When every other woman in Peking left her home and repaired to the British legation, Mrs. Chamot remained by her husband, with a rifle in her hand, and took her regular hours of watching at the loopholes of the barricade erected across Legation street, between the Hotel de Peking and the German legation. Mr. Chamot started a bakery in his hotel, and daily had the Chinese bake hundreds of loaves of good brown bread, with which he supplied many hungry mouths at the English, French, and German legations.

There is no building left standing in Peking that has as many shell-holes in it as the northern two-story building of this hotel. Any one visiting the structure immediately after the relief, and before the débris had been at all cleared, would scarcely believe that a brave American woman had lived there for sixty days unharmed. Her hairbreadth escapes were every-day occurrences. When the Belgian party were surrounded in Chang Hsin Tien, before the close siege commenced, Mr. and Mrs. Chamot, with a small party armed with rifles, went out from Peking and rescued them.

They were in several sorties to the north cathedral before the close siege, and in many more after the close siege had begun. Every day they were under fire in crossing the bridge between their hotel and the British legation, as they brought over the bread that was so eagerly looked for.

After some shells had burst in the baking-room, and killed one and severely wounded others of the Chinese bakers, Mrs. Chamot, rifle in hand, held the coolies to their work while her husband served with the guards.

Mr. Chamot was wounded in the hand by a Boxer spear, but never lost ten minutes' work on that account, going around with his hand tied up, and yet using it whenever occasion required. His bravery was to the point of recklessness, and the wonder is he was not killed. That his country and other nations, especially the French, will substantially recognize his services is surely to be expected.

# Chapter X

An attendant to a Confucian priest

WHILE we were besieged in the legations we were quite unaware of anything going on in the city outside of us until July 18, after the so-called truce, when we paid a native a large sum to smuggle into the compound copies of the Peking "Gazette," the government organ, of the dates of June 13 to July 19, inclusive. The translations of such parts as relate to the Boxers or foreigners that follow show: first, the duplicity of the Empress in apparently trying to suppress the Boxers prior to the declaration of war, June 19; second, her open encouragement in edicts from that date until the defeat of her armies at Tientsin under Generals Sung Ching, Ma Yu Kun and Nieh Shih Cheng, July 17; and third, her immediate turning around and attempting to curry favor by denouncing the Boxers in the edicts of July 18 and 19. While trying her best to murder all the foreign ministers, she was having her own ministers abroad inform the countries to whom they were accredited that the foreign ministers were perfectly safe here.

The edicts speak for themselves, and are an eloquent appeal to the foreign powers never to allow this most treacherous woman, or any other Manchu for that matter, to occupy the throne of China.

"June 13.—Edict: Two days since a member of the Japanese legation, the clerk in chancery, was murdered by desperadoes [her own soldiers in government uniform] outside the Yung Ting gate. We were exceedingly grieved to learn of this.

"The officials of our neighboring nations on duty in Peking should receive our protection in every possible way, particularly in such times as the present [when we are planning to kill them all at once], when every exertion must be used, because desperadoes are as thick as bees.

"We have repeatedly commanded the various local officials to secure the most perfect quiet in their districts, yet in spite of these

ENTRANCE TO THE IMPERIAL UNIVERSITY OF PEKING
Among the notable buildings that were destroyed by the Boxers was the Imperial University of Peking. To the noble work performed within its walls can be attributed much of the rapid rise of the "progressive" or "New China" party, with whom the Emperor seemed to be so thoroughly in accord until his power was subordinated to that of the Empress.

orders we have this case of murder of the Japanese chancellor occurring in the very capital of the Empire.

"The civil and military officials have been too remiss in not clearing their districts of bad characters, or arresting the proper persons, so we hereby set a limit of time for the arrest and punishment of such criminals [time not stated]. Should the time expire without a successful search for the guilty, then the responsible official will be given a penalty. [In other words, if the murderer of the Japanese is not discovered before we drive all the foreigners out, and the plot fails because of this premature murder giving it away, somebody will have to pay for it.]"

"Edict No. 2: The Boxer desperadoes have recently been causing trouble in the neighborhood of the capital, and finally Peking has become involved.

"We have a number of times issued edicts in explicit terms ordering the military commanders on duty near the capital to put an end to these disturbances. Notwithstanding which, cases of murder and arson are reported, and bad characters are circulating malicious rumors under pretense that they are only revenging themselves on converts.

"The result is that our good soldiers have become involved, and do not hesitate to disregard our commands; at the same time they believe these men leagued together to commit arson and murder, and suffer themselves to be misled by them.

"Good citizens most of all desire to stimulate patriotism, and one would like to know when in the history of the world has there ever been a strong nation made so by condoning anarchy among the people. We know, since investigating, that among the ranks of the Boxers there are many bandits and desperadoes, who have vied with one another in disgraceful acts of looting and robbery.

"We have already ordered Kang Yi and others to proceed to the various country districts, and acquaint each and all with our virtuous intentions, so that there may be tranquillity. Let Boxers who have already entered into league disband and be quiet. It is obvious that the various cases of robbery and murder which have occurred are the work of traitors.

"We shall believe no man a bad citizen unless caught red-handed in crime. But really bad characters must be rooted out, and from now on no mercy will be shown such. We order General Sung Ching to command General Ma Yu Kun to come with all speed to the capital, and make strenuous efforts to arrest all desperadoes in the region about Peking. It is important that only ringleaders be seized, but the subordinates may be allowed to scatter.

"It is strictly forbidden that the military make use of this as a means of causing trouble. Our hope is that the land may be cleared of traitors, and the country be at peace."

This edict really means that Ma Yu Kun was to come to Peking, to seize converts, and his soldiers were to avoid any conflict with the Boxers.

"June 19: Recently there has grown up much dissension between the people generally and the Christian converts. Rumors of all kinds have been rife, and irresponsible people have seized the opportunity to burn and rob.

"It is certain that the foreign ministers ought to be protected. [Which means the rumors were that they were to be murdered with government sanction.]

"Yung Lu is ordered to detail his own soldiers and exert his authority in person in east Legation street and vicinity to secure their protection. He must not be lax.

"Should the foreign ministers and their families prefer to temporarily retire to Tientsin, he must see they are protected *en route* [when Baron von Ketteler left the legation walls the following day to visit the tsung-li-yamen he was murdered by these 'protection guards']; but as the railway is not now in working, and if they go by cart-road it would be difficult to secure their safety, they would do better perhaps to abide here in peace as heretofore [we had been under fire for six days at intervals] until the railroad is repaired, and then act as they see fit. Respect this."

"June 21.—Edict: From the foundation of this dynasty, foreigners in China have always been kindly treated. [A tremendous lie.]

"In Tao Kuang and Hsien Feng's time they were granted the privilege of trading, and they then asked permission to propagate their religion, which request was reluctantly granted. At first they were submissive to Chinese control, but for the last thirty years they have taken advantage of China's forbearance to encroach on our territory and trample our people under foot while demanding our wealth.

"Every concession made by China only increased their reliance upon force. They constantly oppressed the people, insulted the gods and sages, and so caused the most burning indignation among the populace. Hence came about the burning of the chapels and slaughter of converts by the patriotic militia [the Boxers].

TEMPLE OF HEAVEN, WHERE THE EMPEROR PRAYED
One of the most imposing temples of China; perhaps the most important, since it was the Emperor's place of worship before he abandoned the capital.

"The throne was anxious to avoid conflict, and issued edicts ordering the protection of the legations and enjoining pity for the converts. Boxers and converts were declared equally the children of the empire in our decrees, in the hope of obliterating the existing feud between them.

"Extreme kindness was shown to the foreigners from a distance. But these foreigners knew no gratitude, and increased their demands.

"A dispatch was yesterday received, sent by the French consul, Du Chaylard, calling on us to deliver into their care the Taku forts, otherwise they would take them by force. This threat showed their aggressive spirit.

"We have in all matters of international intercourse always shown ourselves courteous in the extreme. But they, calling themselves civilized states, have disregarded right and are relying solely upon force.

"We have reigned now nearly thirty years, treating our subjects as our children, and being honored by them as a deity, and, too, we have been the constant recipient of the gracious favor of the Empress Dowager. [This edict pretends to come from the Emperor alone, evidently.]

"Moreover, our ancestors and the gods have answered our prayer, so that there has never been as at present such a universal manifestation of loyalty and patriotism.

"We have, with tears, announced a war in our ancestral shrine, because we feel it is better to commence a struggle than to seek further means of self-protection, involving as it does eternal disgrace.

"All our officials, high and low, are of the same mind, and there have assembled without our call several hundred thousand patriotic militia [Boxers], with many who are yet but children, glad to carry a spear in defense of their country [young ruffians who looted and murdered all the respectable native residents as well as officials who did not fly from Peking before the Boxers entered in any numbers].

"The foreigners rely upon crafty schemes, but our trust is in heaven's justice. They depend on violence, we on humanity [such as killing women and children by the hundreds at the south cathedral], not to speak of the righteousness of our cause.

"Our provinces are more than twenty in number, our population over 400,000,000; so it will not be difficult to vindicate our dignity."

The decree further requests people with money to subscribe assistance, promising official recognition for it, and also offers large rewards for those who distinguish themselves in action, as well as threats for those who are dilatory or cowardly, urging all to exert themselves continually in the good work—exterminating alike foreigners and converts.

"June 24.—Decree: Yesterday shops and residences in Tung Tan Pailou street and Ch'ang Au street were looted by militia with arms [Boxers]. This is a serious matter, so we ordered Yung Lu to depute officers to arrest the offenders. Eleven from one division and twenty-three from another division were arrested and executed on the spot, the public witnessing the executions.

"We now command the general officers of the various divisions to give strict orders to their subordinates that the braves are to be kept in order. Should these occurrences be repeated, martial law will be declared. If the officers commanding screen the offenders, instead of rigorously enforcing the laws, they will be examined, and if found guilty severely punished.

"The military governor of the city is hereby commanded to arrest all desperadoes creating disturbances and execute them on the spot. Show no mercy."

A second decree, same date, says:

"The board of revenue is hereby ordered to give Kang Yi two hundred bags of rice as provisions for distribution among the Boxers." A third decree:

"Members of our people comprised in the Boxer organization are scattered in all parts of the region around the metropolis and Tientsin, and it is right they should have superintendents over them. We appoint, therefore, Prince Chuang and Assistant Grand Secretary Kung Yi to be in general command, and also order Ying Nien brigade-general of the left wing, and Tsai Lan, temporarily acting as a brigade commander of the right wing, to act in cooperation with them.

"We command Wen Yui, adjutant-general of the Manchu army, to be a brigadier-general.

"All members of the Boxer society are exerting their utmost energies for the imperial family, so we must not be behind them in harboring hatred and revenge for our enemies. It is our confident hope and desire that the wishes of each and all may be successfully consummated, and to this end it is important that every energy be put forth, nothing lacking. Respect this."

"June 27.—Edict: An edict appeared yesterday directing, as a stimulus to exertion, discriminating rewards to be given to the various army corps that have distinguished themselves [by looting?] in the metropolitan district. Now that the left wing of the army, under command of Sung Ching, have in sectional divisions marched to the capital, let 100,000 taels be equally divided among the men, and let the men be fully instructed that they are to keep good order in the capital."

An edict was also issued commanding the viceroy of Chihli to retake if possible the Taku forts, and to prevent the foreign troops (the allied armies) from creeping northward. Also another ordering the distribution of 100,000 taels each to the Boxers and troops throughout the Metropolitan district.

"June 28.—Edict: A censor of the central city memorializes the throne requesting the distribution of government rice. He observes that the patriotic Boxers had recently been slaying and burning the converts, and that the markets are greatly disturbed, so that not only the lower classes have lost their means of livelihood, but some of the middle classes are also suffering want. Rather than allow the ranks of the criminal classes to be swollen, let a distribution of food be made by imperial bounty.

"Referring to various precedents, he asks imperial authority for the issue of rice, and that 2,000 taels silver be allowed for expenses.

"He states that on the night of the 16th of June there was a fire in the neighborhood of the Chien Men, accompanied by pillage, and much alarm created. Officials took to flight and shops closed. On the 21st of June an inn in the native city was robbed, and nine persons were caught and beheaded on the spot. On the 25th (Sunday), villains pretending to be soldiers surrounded an official's residence in Second street near the inspectorate-general of customs [probably Marquis Tseng's] and entirely stripped it, shooting wantonly three servants.

"Memorialist and his colleagues will do their best to keep order; but he requests that the throne direct the imperial princes and high officers in command of the Boxers to order arrested any brigands committing robberies. And that the same princes and high officers who command soldiers should see that amongst their corps also there are no false soldiers acting in their true character as bandits, committing acts of pillage."

"June 28. — A censor having complained of acts of brigandage in the capital, we hereby command the princes and ministers in command of the Boxers to instruct their subordinates to arrest all guilty parties and execute them on the spot."

"July 1. — Edict: General preparations are being made for war. Owing to telegraphic communication being interrupted, the courier service, which has fallen into disuse, must be revived. Yu Lu, viceroy of Chihli, is directed to send out courier spies in every direction to obtain exact information of the movements of our enemies."

On the same date a second edict says:

"The members of the Boxer society began by taking as their motto, 'Loyalty and courage.' We consequently expected they would do great service in expelling the oppressors. But Peking and vicinity has witnessed many acts of wanton pillage and murder by bad characters pretending to be Boxers. If no strict distinction is drawn, internal dissension will be added to foreign war, and the state of the country will be unenviable.

"Tsai Hsun, in charge of the Boxers, is hereby ordered to keep the members of his organization in strict subjection to discipline, and to expel pretenders who are in the ranks only to make trouble. Bodies of brigands, of no matter what name, must be dealt with as brigands and have no mercy shown them."

"July 27. — Edict: From the time of the propagation of foreign religions up to the present, there has been much ill-feeling between converts and non-converts. This is all the result of faulty administration on the part of the local officials, which has given rise to lasting feuds.

"The fact remains that converts are still the children of the empire, and among them are undoubtedly some good, worthy people, only they have been led into error by false doctrines, having been misled by the missionaries, and have committed many misdeeds. They still hold to their false beliefs, and an irreconcilable hatred has sprung up between the people and the converts.

"The throne is now recommending every Boxer to render loyal and patriotic service against the enemies of his country, so that the whole population may be of one mind.

"We now state that the converts are, equally with Boxers, subjects, and must follow the rules laid down for all or be destroyed. If they will change their tenets and recant, we can see no reason why they should not be allowed to escape the net. The viceroys and governor-generals are therefore enjoined to issue the following proclamation: 'All converts who recant their former errors, and give themselves up to the authorities, shall be allowed to reform, and the past shall be ignored. The public must be notified of this and each case will be settled by the local officials, according to regulations to be promulgated later on.'

[A nice trap to find out all the converts and exterminate them.]

"As hostilities have now commenced between China and the

foreign nations, the missionaries must be driven away at once, so that they may give no trouble. But it is necessary that they be granted protection *en route*. The provincial authorities must attend to all such within their jurisdiction. Let this be done speedily and with no carelessness."

"July 8.—Edict: The posts about Tientsin are of extreme importance, and troops are being massed there for their defense. The seventy-two fire companies, aggregating over 10,000 men, all animated by a spirit of patriotism, would, if united to the Boxers, greatly swell the strength of our opposition and surely turn the edge of the enemy. Respect this."

"July.—Edict: We appoint Li Hung Chang viceroy of Chihli and superintendent of northern trade [the G. O. M.'s old post]. As the guarding of Tientsin is now of utmost importance, we direct that until Li Hung Chang's arrival Yu Lu, in concert with Prince Ching, consult as to the best measures to be taken. Pending the change of officials, there must be no slackening of responsibility."

The edict of July 12 relates the conduct of General Nieh Shih Cheng, commanding the foreign-drilled troops from Lu Tai, and censures him, but states he died bravely at the head of his soldiers on July 11.

On July 15 Tung Fang, acting governor of Shansi, in a memorial, quotes the following decree transmitted to him by the privy council on June 20:

"A quarrel has broken out between China and foreign nations, and it is difficult to see how matters can be arranged. The viceroys and governors have all been the recipients of imperial favor, and it is now their manifest duty to use every effort to make return, and to lay before us the detail according to the respective circumstances of their several provinces, schemes for the selection of generals, drilling of soldiers, and plans for properly paying them. They must also suggest plans for safeguarding the borders of the country from the aggression of foreigners, as well as see that reinforcements be sent to the aid of the capital in order that no harm befall the dynasty. It is very plain that the situation hinges on the zealous united cooperation of the viceroys and governors that the situation be saved. It is our earnest expectation that full assistance will be given, as is needed in a crisis of this importance. This decree must be published everywhere with the speed its nature demands."

"July 18. — Edict: [Commencing now to hedge, and to negotiate with the foreign ministers still penned up in the British legation. This is after the defeat of the imperial armies at Tientsin]. The reason for the fighting between China and foreign nations sprung from a disagreement between the people and the Christian converts. [That is, the Christian converts objected to being murdered and pillaged wholesale by their heathen neighbors.]

"We could but enter upon war when the Taku forts were taken. Nevertheless, the government is not willing lightly to break off the friendly relations which have existed. We have repeatedly issued orders to protect the ministers of the various countries, and have also ordered the protection of missionaries in the various provinces.

"The fighting has not yet been very extensive, and there are still many merchants of the various countries within our domains. All alike should be protected.

"It is hereby ordered that the generals and governors shall find out wherever there still exist merchants or missionaries, and still protect them according to the provisions of the treaties without the least carelessness. [For nearly a month after this the Empress kept ministers, missionaries, and merchants under the almost constant fire of her troops within two miles of her residence, where she could not but hear every gun fired at them.]

"Last month the chancellor of the Japanese legation was killed. This was most unexpected. Before the case was settled, the German minister was killed. Suddenly meeting this affair caused us great grief. We ought rigorously to seek the murderers and punish them.

"Excepting the fighting at Tientsin, the prefect of Shun Tien Fu, with the governor-general of this province, must command the officers under them to examine what foreigners have been causelessly killed, and what property destroyed, and report the same, that all may be settled together.

"The vagabonds who have been burning houses, robbing, and killing these many days have produced a terrible state of chaos. We order that the viceroy and military officials clearly ascertain the circumstances and unite in reducing confusion to order. Promulgate this decree in such manner that all may know."

"July 19.—Extract from a memorial by Chang Shun: 'Your slave has examined into what has happened recently in the whole region south of the imperial domain in stirring up trouble that has resulted in the destruction of railways and telegraphs, and a morbid chaotic madness seems to possess the masses. Lately a telegram arrived saying warships of all nations had arrived, opened war, captured the Taku forts, and Tientsin was in extreme peril. The Boxers are responsible for all this trouble. The whole world has witnessed our sorrowful condition, troubles alike within and without. The hundreds of millions of taels of silver gathered from three provinces to erect the railroads have been wiped out completely in the destruction of the road by the Boxers in the twinkling of an eye. Who is responsible for the Boxers?' " [Answer—The Empress Dowager and Prince Tuan, both befooled by General Tung Fu Hsiang.]

"July 28.—Yung Lu is granted the privilege of riding in a sedan chair with two bearers within the walls of the imperial palace and inside of the Wan gate."

# Chapter XI

*NOW WHAT?*

One of the many famous temple gates with which China abounds

AND now what? Peking has been relieved, the city is full of soldiers of the allied armies, the Empress and her court have fled westward, and the capital has fallen. Will China be partitioned and divided among her conquerors, or will she be allowed to exist as China under another monarch? Russia undoubtedly wants immediate possession of Manchuria and Chihli, with, very likely, Shansi and Shensi. Japan is quite amenable to further additions to her own territory, and England, although disclaiming any covetous feeling, is believed by a great many of her friends, and all of her enemies, to desire control of the Yangtze valley.

Germany, France, and Italy are all discussing the slice that they desire, and only Uncle Sam has finished his task and wants to go home.

But is his task finished? What about the missionaries murdered in Paoting Fu? Since being relieved, we have heard of the murder, with shocking mutilation, at Paoting Fu, of Mr. and Mrs. Simcox and their three children, of Dr. George Yardley Taylor, of

Dr. and Mrs. Hodge, of Mr. Bagnall and his family, of Mr. Pitkin, Miss Morrill, and Miss Gould. Is Paoting Fu to be allowed to remain on the face of the earth?

And what about Yu Hsien, governor now of Shansi, who had all the foreigners in his province brought into his yamen and murdered before his eyes? Is he to live? No, never. If there exists in America to-day one individual who counsels the return of the troops until the atoning blood of all the leaders and instigators of this awful crime has been poured out, may he be cursed forever.

The work is not yet complete. The Empress Dowager, Prince Tuan, Prince Chuang, Yu Hsien, Tung Fu Hsiang, Chung Chi, Chung Li, Hsu Tung, Kang Yi, Chi Hsiu, Duke Lan, and Na Tung must each and all be brought to the block, with as many of their followers as possible, before the blood of innocent American women and children will cease to cry from the ground for vengeance on their savage, bloody murderers.

Then and only then let America claim indemnity for the property of her citizens that has been destroyed, and retire from the carcass that the other nations will undoubtedly fight over.

If China is to be partitioned, it may injure our trade or it may increase it, but it is not worth our fighting for, when we shall be sure to obtain a great deal of it under any circumstances. It may be best that our troops should remain here during the discussion of the question, but they should not be used in any event.

It is easier to say what should not be done than what should. A few "should nots" like the following will indicate perhaps what might be done:

1. Boxer leaders should not be pardoned.
2. Indemnities should not remain unpaid for years.
3. Manchu banner pensions should not continue.
4. Manchu sovereignty should not remain.
5. Manchu governors should not continue in or hold office.
6. Tribute rice should not be received.
7. Imperial maritime customs should not at present be changed.

8. An entirely native cabinet should not exist.

9. Women's feet should not be bound.

10. Cues should not be worn.

11. Christianity should not be forced on the people.

12. Priests and pastors should not be allowed in yamens.

13. Arms and weapons should not be imported, manufactured, or allowed to be owned by natives.

At the present moment Boxers are practicing in all directions at a distance of from twenty-five to thirty miles from Peking. All of the leaders of the movement are at large, and Prince Ching has returned to Peking to try and arrange a peace. Now what?

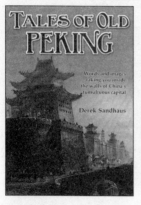
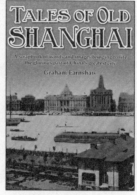

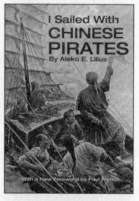

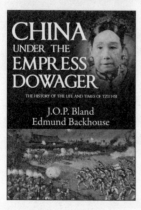
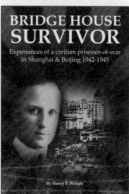